50 WAYS TO BRING OUT THE Smarts IN YOUR KID

MARGE KENNEDY

Peterson's

Princeton, New Jersey

Portions of 46: My Child's Learning Style *originally appeared in* Good Housekeeping, *September 1995.*

Some of the material in 48: Parent-Teacher Conferences *appeared in* Better Homes and Gardens, *November 1995.*

Visit Peterson's at http://www.petersons.com

Library of Congress Cataloging-in-Publication Data

Kennedy, Marge M., 1950–
    50 ways to bring out the smarts in your kid / Marge Kennedy.
      p.   cm.
    Includes bibliographical references.
      ISBN 1-56079-590-5
     1. Education—Parent participation—United States. 2. Home and school—United States. 3. Active learning.
    4. Child rearing—United States. I. Title.
    LB1048.5.K45   1996
    370.19′31′0973—dc20   96-44653
                                                                 CIP

Editorial direction by Carol Hupping
Production supervision by Bernadette Boylan
Copyediting by Sandra Noelle Smith
Proofreading by Joanne Schauffele

Composition by Gary Rozmierski
Creative direction by Linda Huber
Interior design by Cynthia Boone

Printed in the United States of America

10 9 8 7 6 5 4 3 2 1

CONTENTS

Introduction

As parents, we are of two minds when it comes to judging the "smarts" of our kids. On the one hand, we know they're brilliant—sometimes simply because they're ours and sometimes because they have amazed us with their insights. On the other hand, we may wonder why that brilliance doesn't always glow in the classroom or why he or she makes poor choices in daily life. Perhaps most importantly, we want to know what we can do to ensure that our kids are given the opportunity to grow into the best people they can be.

How can we help them revel in their childhoods, free from undue school and social stresses, while encouraging them to buckle down so that they can bring home grades that reflect their academic promise and behave in ways that reflect their best selves? How can we help them concentrate on the basics and still ensure that they maintain their creative spirits? How do we impart the values that will serve them and society when we see those values in flux? How do we define success?

The struggle to achieve does not belong just to our children, of course. We parents are supposed to bring out the best in our kids even while we're holding down full-time jobs, volunteering to keep the school and community afloat, and getting by on less sleep than we'd ever dreamed possible. And the biggest job—raising human beings, those ever-changing bundles of energy, feelings, likes, dislikes, and idiosyncracies—is a full-time job all its own. Moreover, we want our children's growing-up years, as well as our own time with them, to be joyous, not simply productive. We need help.

This book grew out of my own pursuit of that help. As a writer and editor of educational materials for parents and children for more than twenty years, I have been immersed in much of the research that has affected the ways in which children are taught and the assumptions about the ways in which they learn. Over the years, I've seen the emphasis shift from back-to-basics, content-based philosophies to individualized, process-centered ones and back again. Every trend and tradition has some merit—and some loss. All focused on intellectual and/or psychosocial matters. For a time, preferred theories centered on making kids feel good, limiting their frustrations, and moving them along at a comfortable pace, whether or not they were learning anything other than feeling good. In my career, I became adept at writing materials that purported to teach academic skills for children from nursery school through high school. Some were, no doubt, successful in that they did help children grasp the concepts being addressed. But, after becoming the parent of a now 8-year-old third-grader, I became increasingly frustrated with the business I was in. The many books and articles I'd been reading and writing began to feel sterile—clinically useful and enlightening but a bit soulless and heartless, assuming, I think, that learning and life itself took place from the neck up.

What I came to see was that learning involves more than absorbing information. It requires an attitude that says, "I can do it!" It takes time and energy. No teaching methods, no books, no assessments matter as much as helping a child *choose to learn* and then *giving her the tools to do it*.

In researching this book, I spoke with hundreds of educators, parents, and kids, eliciting the best advice on enhancing learning at home and at school in academic, social, and deeply personal ways. This book is planned for parent readers of normal kids (and here, "normal" means just about every kid, from the hesitant learner to the exceedingly motivated). These "50 Ways" are the routines and attitudes that parents and kids can integrate into their everyday lives, rather than a compendium of specific projects that aim to increase aptitude in any particular subject.

Its goal is not necessarily to create "A" students, but "A" people, and to help families create an environment that enhances learning across a broad range of disciplines. Hand-in-hand with that goal is helping parents and kids work effectively within the school environment and within the strictures that often can seem at odds with a child's abilities and/or natural learning style. Finally, the aim of this book is to help parents and kids put the academic process into its proper perspective—as an essential *part* of the business of growing up, but not the sum total of the experience.

It's my hope that *50 Ways to Bring Out the Smarts in Your Kid* will serve you and your children in ways that help make the learning process more fun and more of a natural part of your family's everyday routines.

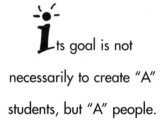

*I*ts goal is not necessarily to create "A" students, but "A" people.

Part 1:

Creating a Learning Environment at Home

1 Embracing the Real Child

Every parent gives birth to two children—the one who actually arrives and the one who is the stuff of dreams. That child, the imagined child, enters the world fully capable of sleeping through the night, reading the encyclopedia by age 3, and performing concertos by age 6, while investing the book royalties from her earlier novel that will fund her college education (which she'll complete by age 12).

This child needs no parents.

The real child, on the other hand, is perfectly human and humanly imperfect. At age 3, she wants to wear a ballet costume to play in the snow; at 7, she could care less that she left her backpack in school for the third day in a row and therefore can't do her homework *again*; and at age 12, dyes her hair orange with Jell-O on a dare.

This child needs you.

It's a rare parent who wants to change the color of her child's eyes, yet many of us want to change our children's fundamental natures. We want our daydreaming, head-in-the-clouds child to remember to take out the trash. We want our witty conversationalist to ace Friday's math test. We even want our nose-in-a-book child to learn how to toss a ball and make friends more easily. We want well-rounded, happy children who are good at many things. But most real children are not good at all things all the time. Meanwhile, that imagined child malingers like an annoying houseguest, intruding on our interactions with our real child, causing frustration all around. What can we do to meet the needs of the real child? How do we lock the imagined child away somewhere, where she won't compete with this less-than-perfect kid?

Like most issues of parenting, changing our kids begins with making some changes within ourselves. The first step is to let go of our own sense of failure for not living up to the ideal of the imagined parent—the mother or father we were going to be before we had kids; the parent who never loses her temper, who patiently answers all questions, and who bakes wholesome goodies every morning before breakfast. We need to accept that parenting is an imprecise science and that our own imperfections sometimes serve our children well. The job *requires* that we make mistakes. It involves discovery, not certainty. The more comfortable we can become in our role as confident explorers of this world with our children, the easier it becomes to bring out the smarts in them. As the grown-ups in this exploration, of course, we have an obligation to provide the map, to offer safe refuge when necessary, to lead, and eventually, to nudge our children along toward independence.

The birth experience itself should, but doesn't always, provide the wake-up call we need, the signal that we're in for a bit more than we bargained for when it comes to accepting the realities of being a parent. If your child isn't quite living up to expectations, it might be because the expectations are out of sync with the child's fundamental being. To enjoy the real child:

Like most issues of parenting, changing our kids begins with making some changes within ourselves.

Resist the temptation to compare your child to your remembered self at your child's age.

Be realistic. Ask yourself, "Is my child's behavior similar to the behavior of other children his age?" If your 10-year-old dawdles over homework, is his dawdling much more pronounced than that of other kids his age? To find out, talk to other parents and teachers who may be able to assure you that though his dawdling is driving you crazy, other 10-year-olds' dawdling is also driving *their* parents crazy. Resist comparing your kid to the one or two who don't dawdle. (Those kids probably are doing something else to drive their parents nuts.)

Don't count on memories. Also resist the temptation to compare your child to yourremembered self at your child's age. Nature endows us all with selective memory, and when we think we're recalling ourselves competently tackling our homework at age 10, the chances are that we're really remembering someone else (or ourselves a few years later). A good reality check on your own true record is to go back and look over those old report cards. If your mother doesn't have them in an accessible shoebox, your old school will have them. (They're part of that "permanent record" you were taught to fear.)

Practice patience. It's tempting to expend energy on fixing things (including our kids) now. We worry that each bad habit or each misstep will blossom into a bed of weeds. Most won't. Sometimes the best reaction to a child's imperfection is to do nothing for the time being. Remember that children are busy learning lots of things and that they can't bring all their efforts equally to each task. A child who's working through the social issues brought on by puberty is naturally distracted from algebra.

Overlook the little stuff. I recall being at a 7-year-old's birthday party and becoming livid with my daughter for chewing on her fingers throughout the celebration. The habit was driving me nuts. A friend, overhearing me correct her, suggested that I look around first. Her own son was chewing on his shirt cuff. Another girl was picking her nose. One was busy hair twirling. Not one party guest, it turned out, was practicing exemplary public behaviors. Why was I expecting my daughter to be perfect? That occasion taught me that it wasn't necessary to hover and correct each and every misdemeanor.

Understand the dynamics. Sometimes, coming to terms with how we *really* feel about a child is difficult to do. We know we're supposed to love and cherish everything about our precious kid even if he has zits and is more stubborn than a grape-juice stain. But not every parent and every child are a perfect match at every stage of their mutual growth. Sometimes, differences (or similarities) in personalities upset the parent-child relationship. An athletic parent may have difficulty enjoying a child's bookishness. The same child's love of books would be seen in a more positive light by a parent who also enjoys reading. The more opportunities we create to hang out with our kids, doing what they like to do and inviting them to share those activities we enjoy, the better able we are to appreciate their unique talents and interests.

Be positive in your assessments. Work at naming the things about your child that you truly admire. If your 6-year-old struggling reader has you at wit's end over his slowness to distinguish a "b" from a "d," let him know that not everyone can kick a soccer ball as well as he can. Remind him of his strengths at least as often as you work with him to gain

*U*nconditional love is every child's birthright.

•

9

strength in areas that do not come as easily for him. Also, rephrase to yourself as well as to others his perceived shortcomings. A "hyperactive" kid can also be called "energetic." A "daydreaming" child can be described as "thoughtful." Describing your child as "challenging" to a teacher (instead of calling him a "real pain in the butt," for instance) gives the teacher a positive way to see him, too, and puts the issue of rising to the challenge in the teacher's hands. Everyone, including your child, needs good PR.

Demonstrate your approval. It would be wrong to show approval for every *behavior* a child exhibits; it would be equally wrong not to show your full approval for the *person* a child is. Unconditional love is every child's birthright.

READ MORE ABOUT IT

The best books to help parents understand normal child development are contained in the series developed by Louise Bates Ames and Frances L. Ilg of the Gesell Institute of Child Development. The titles are *Your One-Year Old, Your Two-Year-Old, Your-Three-Year Old, Your-Four-Year-Old, Your Five-Year-Old, Your Six-Year-Old, Your Seven-Year-Old, Your Eight-Year-Old, Your Nine-Year-Old,* and *Your Ten- to Fourteen-Year Old.* (Delta Books)

2 Establishing Rituals and Routines

At the end of the cut-loose sixties, I and a few hundred other questers gathered on a mountainside in California (of course) for a spiritual service of sorts, put together by the local gurus. The rite was designed, on the spot it seemed, to include elements of both Eastern and Western traditions. The leaders insisted that we abstain from following any recognizable rituals—no songs, no chanting, no common prayer—nothing that served to bind any groups of us, lest any of us feel excluded. The important thing, we all agreed, was that we do it together. The "it," however, remained undefined and elusive for the hours that we held onto that hillside.

While the brilliant morning sunshine was in itself inspiring, the lack of ritual, the communal guessing about what was to happen next, and the subsequent restlessness of the crowd eroded any sense of community well before noon. Without singing songs that most of us knew or reciting words in harmony, the service soon became not much more than a crowd who happened to be in the same place at the same time.

Families, too—even well-meaning ones—can occupy space together while sharing little else. None of us has all the time, energy, or other resources we need to devote as much attention to each other as we'd like. School schedules, work schedules, and household maintenance seem to conspire to keep our interactions with the people who matter most to us to a functional minimum. But even within the strictures of modern life, parents need to make certain that family members check in with one another in a meaningful way each and every day to remind us regularly of the uniqueness and importance of our particular clan. Giving ourselves and our kids the opportunity to get to know one another well cannot happen by accident. We've got to plan for it. And rather than taking more time from our busy schedules, the establishment of rituals creates time (and good times). As an added bonus, children who grow up in organized homes with established routines tend to do well in school—and in life.

For routines to be effective, they have to involve positive interactions. A routine of bypassing each other in the hallway while eating Twinkies for dinner won't do. To make time for family structure, you may have to spend some time up front creating a schedule and organizing materials until the routines are so established that the mundane chores are done on automatic pilot. On a daily basis:

Eat together. The breakfast and/or dinner table is the best place to share more than a meal. A study reported in early 1996 by Washington University professor Diane Beals, Ed.D., and research associate Patton Tabors at Howard University's Graduate School of Education found that children whose parents expose them to dinner-time conversation score significantly higher on verbal skills and become better readers than kids whose families do not share the dinner-time habit.

> For routines to be effective, they have to involve positive interactions.

Have regular check-ins. Parents and children often pass each other coming and going. In itself, the normal hectic schedule does no harm. But without established meetings and greetings, something important is lost. Enjoy a regular morning send-off, a midday check-in, and an evening reconnection. Working parents and their children need to get in the habit of calling each other at certain times during the day. The routines needn't be elaborate, but they must be consistent.

Read. Parents of preschoolers and kindergarteners usually establish a bedtime reading routine. Unfortunately, once kids begin to read on their own, even haltingly, parents willingly forego partaking in this important ritual. But it's important to remember that childrens' listening abilities far surpass their reading abilities for years after basic literacy emerges. An 8-year-old, for instance, may have difficulty tackling *The Chronicles of Narnia* on her own, but will surely love having this series by C. S. Lewis read aloud to her. Besides boosting the child's vocabulary and appreciation of literature, reading together provides an incredible closeness and peacefulness that few other activities do.

Follow a reasonable daily schedule. Mundane things like going to bed at a certain time each night and getting up after a full dose of required sleep go a long way to giving kids the freedom within safe boundaries that they need. Eating at predictable times and places is essential. Additionally, schoolkids need a regular time and place to accomplish homework, as well as time each day to play and interact with friends and family.

Talk. It's important to get beyond the, "Pick up your socks and do your homework" level of conversation. Share details from your day. Elicit one another's opinions. At the end of the day, verbalize what the day has brought to you and what your hopes are for tomorrow.

Allow for spontaneity. The importance of routine shouldn't be confused with a military approach to family life. While predictability is important, it doesn't negate the pleasure that can be had by occasionally deviating from routine or the gains that come from learning to "go with the flow." (And if there weren't a regular routine, deviation from it would be impossible.) When friends drop by unexpectedly, for example, it's appropriate to respond by welcoming them rather than sending them on their way because seeing them wasn't part of your plans. So much of the unexpected, both good and bad, will happen in the course of your children's lives that learning to alter their plans and to work with change are absolutely necessary.

Make peace and express thankfulness. Don't let the day end without letting your children know that you are grateful for their place in your life.

S hare details from

your day.

3 Creating Memories

Beyond the everyday rituals that help define a family, the rhythms of the week and the year offer opportunities to enrich one another. Outside our normal routines, there is a larger canvas on which to paint our lives. Weekly (or otherwise regularly):

Set aside a time to reflect. Life is noisy. Include some regular routines that celebrate quiet and reflection. For many families, this includes regularly attending religious services. Others find renewal in a Saturday-morning hike through the woods, a lazy Sunday-morning brunch, or a drive through the country.

Join in community activities. Sharing your family time with others in your community strengthens both your family and the community. Attend local cultural events, take part in scouting or Little League activities, engage in volunteer work. Let your children see that giving of themselves to others is enriching and deeply satisfying.

Discuss family operations. In addition to the daily chats you have with your kids about chores, homework, and life in general, set aside a specific time to review family

Include some regular routines that celebrate quiet and reflection.

15

business such as allowances (time for a raise?), changes in routines, upcoming birthday parties or vacation plans, and anything else that needs attention.

Work alongside one another. Kids need to learn how to shop, fix the car, and perform the other things we do to keep the family running. We need to know what they're learning in school and elsewhere and what matters to them socially. Make a point of inviting your child to help you accomplish the things you must. Offer to help him with what he needs to do. Oftentimes, the best conversations occur during these mundane circumstances.

Everyone needs to be celebrated.

Limit time wasters. Stay away from malls and other spirit-deadening hangouts. Limit television viewing. Make phone calls from work or after the kids are in bed. Eliminate superfluous possessions that require storing, cleaning, fixing, or moving.

Have fun. This may seem obvious, but many of us go weeks on end without having a good time together. Rent a funny movie and whip up a batch of popcorn to enjoy together. Invite another family over. Go to an amusement park or on a bike ride together. Practice card tricks to perform for one another. Learn a new joke. Laugh.

Celebrate each other. Don't let birthdays, anniversaries, job and school promotions, and other accomplishments slip by unnoticed. Everyone needs to be celebrated. Involve children not only in the planning of their own birthday parties, but in planning yours, too. Before proceeding with this year's holiday rituals, for instance, find out what they enjoyed most about last year's that they don't want to miss this year and what parts, if any, they'd like to change.

Create your own special holiday. The calendar provides many potential celebrations, and you and your family can pick out one to make truly your own. One family might choose to throw an annual St. Patrick's Day party; another may organize the neighborhood's annual Fourth of July picnic. Yours may prefer to have an annual celebration all your own, such as Wacky Friday, an annual event on which you and your kids trade responsibilities. Ask the kids for their suggestions.

Vacation together. While costs and time constraints work to keep you and your kids chained to the daily routines, it's essential to break away for a few days or more whenever possible to explore new places. Against a different backdrop, everyone looks a little better. On a recent trip to Tampa/St. Pete, I saw in my daughter a love of nature I'd never really appreciated before. Her sheer delight at swimming inches from a suddenly appearing school of dolphins, her new interest in sea turtles, her ability to know one kind of shell from another all gave me a new perspective on my land-locked city kid.

Record yourselves. Take pictures and/or make videos and tape recordings. Save and display your kids' artwork (at least representative samples from year to year). Show off photos of the immediate and the extended family, including photos of grandparents and great-grandparents. Keeping track of how everyone is evolving is an important way to acknowledge and remember shared experiences.

4 A Safe Haven for Risk Taking

When she was 4, my daughter announced to a visiting playmate that "My mother is perfect." Who was I to argue? I've always wished I'd gotten that remark on tape so that I could play it back to myself in times of self-doubt and play it back to her (with the volume on high) when she questions my wisdom, which she now does with increasing frequency.

On the other hand, sometimes I'm glad for the freedom that this acknowledged imperfection buys me now. Free of having to be better than I am, I can still be really good at this job of being my daughter's mother (most of the time). I've learned to use my experience in raising her successfully so far as a springboard for trying new approaches now and again. Some work; others don't. I'm not quite so terrified of screwing up as I was when I first brought her home. In the same vein, being able to admit that I *have* bungled it gives me a chance to start again. Kids need that freedom, too.

When a toddler stumbles and we refrain from making a big deal over a minor scrape, we teach him that his risk-taking behavior is appropriate and that the risk of falling is worth the payoff of walking. When we marvel over those first steps, we doubly reward his efforts. Each new skill gained by the preschooler is celebrated—first words, first day staying dry, first climb to the top of the jungle gym. No reasonable parent says, "That's nice, but not quite good enough" when a 3-year-old shows off her latest crayoned creation. There's no such thing as a mistake when the process of learning is as valued as the product of learning. Most kids enter school as willing risk takers. After all, they've been armed with years of parental encouragement and their own experiences at taking chances and subsequently gaining new skills.

But as their school careers progress, something changes. Social issues move to the forefront. A child's performance in relation to the performance of others becomes more important to parents and teachers. This introduces a strange new concept to kids—the idea of failure and the subsequent fear of making a mistake. Their once innate confidence in their ability to learn new skills and their pleasure in learning is short-circuited. This is not a natural process. It is a learned response.

We undermine our kids' confidence in their ability to learn with the best of intentions, of course. Afraid perhaps that they won't learn the prescribed skills at the prescribed rate, we push them toward accomplishment in a very narrow range of skills. Sometimes we ask too much too soon, expecting, for example, that our 6-year-old will read fluently just because another 6-year-old has mastered the skill. Or we rush in to save a child from error before she's had a chance to correct herself and to learn from their mistake. We glean over the *process* of discovery and look for results. We're no longer as quick to applaud our child's made-up dance step when the rest of the world is stressing her need to recognize lowercase letters, reduce fractions to their lowest common

There's no such thing as a mistake when the process of learning is as valued as the product of learning.

When parents and teachers react negatively to the experimentation that accompanies new learning experiences, kids can become frightened and thus more careful and less adventurous as they learn.

denominator, or memorize a passage from Shakespeare. Once academic learning enters the picture, a child may experience for the first time the feeling that her work is not good enough and the knowledge that others her age may do certain things better. Or she may learn that what matters most to her, such as drawing or building or playing dress-up, is not necessarily a pursuit that others find important.

As school demands grow larger in the upper grades, there often is even less allowance made for experimentation, especially in areas that don't bear directly on academic accomplishment.

For many kids, the model of other children mastering a new skill prods them along to acquire the same skill—if they are ready to learn it. But when parents and teachers react negatively to the experimentation that accompanies new learning experiences, and when kids are discouraged from learning things that matter to them (but not to you or their teachers, such as skateboarding) kids can become frightened and thus more careful and less adventurous as they learn.

The 6-year-old who writes a backward 6 in answer to "how much is 4 + 2" is immediately corrected even though he shows the correct sum. The 12-year-old who has to stay up late to finish a book report because she got so involved in the challenge of a new computer game is told to limit her energies to her schoolwork. Imagine, if instead, we told the 6-year-old simply that the answer was correct and let the backwardness of the numeral go unaddressed for the moment. That might prod him on to figure out another addition problem. If we acknowledged to the 12-year-old that "you really seem involved in that program," she might be inspired to try to explain it to us. Sure, she may also need some help in organizing her time so that playing her computer games and writing her report both work into her schedule. But the passion to work through the computer challenge needn't be dismissed as useless. It isn't. Not to her.

Ironically, overpraising every effort and accomplishment can also backfire. Kids who are told that they are brilliant again and again become frightened of falling from grace. The high-achieving early reader may be unwilling to swim, since the learning process of swimming will involve more risk taking than she's used to handling. Her efforts in this new area may not result in quick applause. Having to maintain such a high level of performance can be paralyzing.

By interrupting the process of learning, by overresponding to the failures and the successes, we inadvertently teach kids to enjoy only the destination of learning, not the travel experience. We need to counter the loss of enthusiasm that accompanies a perceived or a feared failure, while still helping our kids learn the things they need to know. We need to help them enjoy the ride as much as the arrival. How do we do it? The key is to continue to celebrate the process of learning, not just the end product. Primarily that means allowing for, even welcoming, mistakes. Only a risk taker can make a mistake—or accomplish something incredible. Here are some ways to help your child incorporate the trial-and-error process into the joy of accomplishment:

Allow experimentation. The highway may be the fastest way to get where we're going, but the off-the-beaten-path roads offer more surprises. It's important to let our kids know that the proven means of getting from Point A to Point B is not the only possible route. By learning to take reasonable risks, we're free to find a new way to get to Point B. Or we may discover Point C along the way.

Show that mistakes are part of life. It's easy to think that our kids—especially if they're over age 7 or so—are already too aware of our shortcomings. They are aware of our imperfections, but to a much smaller degree than their protests about us would lead us to believe. In fact, through their teen years, kids believe that we know a lot more than they let on. They need *us* to acknowledge our own fumblings and our own efforts to recover from them. Saying, "I really blew it" when we really blow it allows kids to do the same. It allows for a new starting place. Apologizing when necessary is part of the script, too, as is sincerely trying to make amends when a mistake has been hurtful to someone else.

Limit reactions. A matter-of-fact response to the errors that a learner has made keeps him working toward a goal instead of having to waste energy defending himself. For instance, saying, "Recheck your answer to number 7" after you review your child's math homework is likely to be met with a more positive response than saying, "Number 7 is wrong." Likewise, not going overboard with lavish praise allows her to try something at which she is not yet very good.

Remind kids of the work that precedes accomplishment. Many kids are surprised when they approach a new skill to find that the results aren't what they'd anticipated. For instance, a child whose friend plays the piano may want to learn, too. Then, after one lesson, he wants to give up. What went wrong? Where did that enthusiasm go? What often happens to dampen a child's surge forward is the discovery that learning usually

They need *us* to acknowledge our own fumblings and our own efforts to recover from them.

requires a great deal of work. The friend who plays well put many hours into becoming competent. The same will be true for any new learner. When a child wants to give up soon after starting to learn something new, remind him of those things that he couldn't do at first but mastered after repeated attempts. Show him examples of his early scribbling to remind him of progress in his artwork. Remind him of how much better he can kick a ball now than when he was little. Work out a plan for putting in the required work to achieve the desired result in any new area of study.

Stick to the real issue. Instead of looking to place blame when a child's performance is less than it could be, concentrate on attacking the problem, not the child. A failed spelling test doesn't indicate that a child is stupid or lazy, that the teacher didn't teach, or that your child inherited a faulty spelling gene from your spouse's side of the family. It may mean that he didn't study. It may mean that he didn't study in a way that allowed him to absorb the information. Or it may mean that he needs concentrated help in this subject area. These things can be accomplished with no loss to anyone's sense of self.

Provide opportunities for playfulness. With so much to learn, it's easy for kids and parents both to put a lot of energy into pursuing certain academic skills. But everyone needs unstructured time for creative, experimental play, where the mind voluntarily becomes engaged with its surroundings. An afternoon spent on the beach with no books to read and no toys to play with will lead a child to discover the qualities of sand, the physics behind a sand castle standing or collapsing, the many uses of shells. The child whose mind is free to roam learns to hear what the wind has to say.

5 Communicating Effectively

Parent: How was school today?
Child: Fine.
Parent: What did you do?
Child: Nothing.

Sound familiar? The grand drama of most families was not, alas, written by Shakespeare. That doesn't mean that we, too, can't aspire to great heights in the art of conversation at home. We just have to remember to take turns being orator and audience, and that's hard for many of us.

Conversation is where we humans connect to one another. When the dialog is between adults and kids, each brings something special to the stage. Kids bring questions, wonder, energy, and excitement. Adults bring experience and a larger, more precise vocabulary. How well children develop the art of conversation begins long before they babble their first words. It begins with having their cries answered and their gazes met.

When they know that they're listened to, that we care about keeping the connection alive and vibrant, they continue their quest to communicate in language, mimicking what they hear, bringing meaning to the sounds as they grow.

As parents, we continue to add to the script, giving them more and more words to add to their repertoires. Then comes the day that they're speaking in sentences, saying no, and asking hard questions. For many of us, that's when things can begin to break down. Often, it's when we stop really listening to one another. If we begin to take their rambling for granted, half tuning them out, we risk missing out on being privy to their insights. If we respond to their no's with no's of our own (about as monosyllabic as a conversation can get!), we stop all real communication in its tracks. And if we dismiss some of the many, many questions with no more than an "I don't know," they learn to stop asking. And that would be a real shame. To help make conversation work for you and your child:

Set aside time to talk. Make sure that there's time every day to talk—over a meal, at bedtime, in the car—when there's no other agenda, few interruptions, and where you and each child can get and give some one-on-one attention to one another.

Share your thoughts and elicit your child's opinion. If you're thinking of redecorating your child's bedroom, for example, talk over the possibilities with your child and ask about his preferences. Share your reasons for making the decisions you make about things like voting, taking a certain route to work, or whatever.

Show a real interest in what a child has to say. Make eye contact whenever possible during conversations with your child. Stop whatever else you're doing at those

When the dialog is between adults and kids, each brings something special to the stage.

times he or she wants and needs your full attention. (Keep doing what you're doing, however, on those occasions when your child wants to talk but doesn't want to get too serious. Kids generally hate it when every utterance is latched onto as if it were part of the most important conversation ever to take place. Lighten up. Follow your kid's lead on how much focused attention the conversation needs.) Sometimes a parent can't stop what he or she is doing to give wholehearted attention to what a child has to say at the moment. In that case, tell him that "I really want to hear this, but I can't give you my full attention now." Then set a time when you can listen attentively and keep your appointment.

Draw on what you know matters to your child as a conversation starter.

Focus on life, not on chatter. Lots of times, we put talking before communication. In other words, we fill up the space with useless questions and small talk rather than with any real attempt at connecting. The "How was school today?" question is typical of the lame conversation stopper we easily toss at kids. Instead, draw on what you know matters to your child as a conversation starter. For instance, if you know that your daughter's concerned about a friend who's moving away, invite her to talk about that. "What plans have you and Gabby made for keeping in touch?" might work. Be careful, however, especially with preteens and older kids, not to declare that "I know just how you feel," about anything. Yes, you may know how she feels, but saying so is robbing her of her ability to own those feelings right now.

Tell stories. Most kids love real-life recollections of things that matter to them, such as the day they were born or a funny story about your own childhood. Make up stories, too, with each participant adding a line or two. (One storyteller begins, "It was a dark and stormy night, when suddenly, there was a knock at the door." The next storyteller picks up from there: "I called out, 'Who is it?' but no one answered. . . .") Record the story by writing it down as you go along or by tape recording it. Attend professional storytelling events, including story hour at the library for younger children and more involved events for older kids and parents.

Communication Strategies that Work When You're Angry at Your Child's Behavior

Not all conversation is enlightening. Nor does it always need to be. Sometimes, parents must correct kids' behavior or remind them to do what they must. Choosing your words wisely can make the difference as to whether or not your child hears what you have to say.

Avoid labels. Calling a child "stupid" or "lazy" or using any other attacking language invalidates our authority. A child with even an ounce of selfworth can't listen attentively to anything we have to say after we've dismissed her with insults. Also stick to the present. Instead of saying, "You always . . . ," limit any verbal correction to the here and now. Saying, "You spilled the juice, so now you'll have to help clean it up," beats saying, "There you go again! That's the third time this week that you've been so careless."

Use "I" statements. These are three-part statements that describe a behavior, express your feelings about that behavior, and state the objective consequence of that behavior.

For instance, instead of shouting, "Don't leave your bicycle in the driveway!" say, "When you leave your bicycle in the driveway, I can't see it, and I may run over it when I drive in." Or, "When you tell me something that isn't true, I lose my trust in you, and I will be less likely to believe what you say in the future." That puts the responsibility in the right place and gives the child the opportunity to make the situation right.

Listen reflectively. Listening involves "hearing" a child's body language as well as his words, and reflective listening works well when a child needs words to express his feelings instead of simply acting out. For example, when a child stalks into the room, slamming the door behind him, we might be tempted to say, "Cut that out!" A better response is to say, "I can see that you're angry" and to engage the child in conversation so that he can express verbally what's troubling him.

Respond with—and teach—empathy. This gets right to the child's feelings and is especially useful in helping him validate his feelings while alerting him to the feelings of others. When a child grabs a toy from a sibling, for instance, say, "I know you want that ball right now . . . ," which better prepares him for the second part of your statement, ". . . but you can't grab it from your brother."

Whisper.

READ MORE ABOUT IT

For some great advice on the art of family conversation, read *How to Have Intelligent and Creative Conversations with Your Kids,* by Jane M. Healy, Ph.D. (Doubleday).

6 Listening to Learn

There's so much wisdom we parents are just dying to impart that it's amazing our voices hold up. In a cartoon I have pasted to the refrigerator, a mom is shown spouting a list of directives to her uninterested teen—about twelve lines long. What the teenager hears is "blah, blah, blah." Clearly conversations with our kids don't mean much if either one of us isn't listening. To learn to listen and listen to learn, try these strategies:

Keep speech and vocabulary corrections to a minimum. When a toddler points to a zebra at the zoo and calls it a horse, instead of immediately saying, "No, it's a zebra," try, "It sure looks like a horse. It has four legs like a horse. It has a mane like a horse. But its black and white stripes tell us that it's a zebra." Likewise, when she calls her "shoes" her "foos," there's no need to have her repeat the correct pronunciation for you. Instead offer her a chance to hear you say the word and trust that she'll pick up the standard pronunciation in due time: "Yes, those are your *shoes* and these are my *shoes*."

When a preschooler describes the way he sees the world according to his imagination rather than according to facts, don't rush in to fix things. For instance, when he says that a big flying bug took a bite out of the quarter moon, resist the urge to "correct" his imagining by launching into an explanation of moon phases. Instead invite him to expand upon this wonderful image: "What do you think the moon tastes like? Does the flying bug take bites out of stars, too? If you could fly, where would you go?" Listen for his answers, and if he seems interested in pursuing this line of thought, make up more questions as you go along. Language, and the ideas that language allows us to discuss, grow best in fertile soil. As with toddlers, keep pronunciation corrections to a bare minimum. (If you suspect that your child is having a true language delay, however, talk over the situation with his pediatrician or contact the speech pathology department of your local college or health center to see if remediation is called for.)

For older children, who think far faster than they can speak and who are still absorbing the rules of proper grammar, limit interrupting their talk with admonishments to slow down or speed up or to use proper words. If your child's going too fast or too slow, ignore it most of the time, unless his speed is really interfering with your ability to understand. Then just remind him that you want to understand and that he'll need to adjust his delivery. To correct grammar, repeat what the child says with the right words instead of offering an interrupting correction. For example, when your child relates about a friend that "He don't like soccer," say, "He doesn't like soccer?" giving your child a chance to correct himself the next time. Most importantly, model good speech patterns yourself.

Hold off on correcting the child's character, too, during every conversation. One 12-year-old I know related how she gets so angry at her mother for frequently interrupting her with advice. "Like when I say that I have a test tomorrow, she starts right in about how I need to study, blah, blah, blah, and all and won't even let me finish what I was saying. I didn't tell her about the test so that she could remind me to study. That's ridiculous. I wish she'd just listen before trying to tell me something." Which leads us to . . .

Listen—and keep quieter than you may want. When you're engaged in a conversation with your child, really listen. Sometimes that means asking the right questions or responding to stated opinions with ideas of your own. Sometimes it means being mute. (A 4-year-old friend once asked his mom to "listen with your ears, not with your mouth.") Don't assume all the time that your child wants your advice; often, he just wants your attention.

Don't interrupt or allow others to interrupt. Most parents have brought home the lesson that children are not to interrupt an adult conversation unless it's absolutely essential. Despite training our kids to leave us to our talk, we tend to interrupt them freely or allow others to interrupt our conversations with them with equal ease. It drives kids nuts and rightly so whenever we opt out of a chat with them because something else (a telephone call, another adult entering the room) comes along. We wouldn't do the same with a friend because we simply wouldn't be that rude with a friend whose love and loyalty we don't take for granted. Our kids deserve the same respect.

Likewise, we shouldn't let stray parental thoughts seep into the conversation when those thoughts have nothing whatsoever to do with the content of the conversation. My

Don't assume all the time that your child wants your advice; often, he just wants your attention.

31

daughter reminded me of this recently when she was telling me about her desire to live in the country when she grew up. "I'd have a big deck for picnics and a cow or two in the yard." It would have remained an interesting conversation if I had not jumped in to ask her if she'd put away the books I'd piled on her bed. "Mom!" she said, clearly frustrated with my lack of attention to her dreams, "I hate when you put what I'm telling you into the garbage."

Limit distractions. Turn off the television. Turn on the answering machine to screen calls so that you don't have to jump up in the middle of a sentence. Ask anyone else in the room to give you and your child a moment alone. Make eye contact. When what you have to say can wait a moment, make an appointment, "I want to talk with you. Give me five minutes before dinner after you've finished that project."

Practice listening skills. Play Simon Says and other games that require attentive listening. Try list-making games, in which one player says a word ("Cheese," for example) and the next player adds a related word (e.g. "Cheese, Mouse") and the next player adds another ("Cheese, Mouse, Trap") and see how long the word chain can continue unbroken. Play telephone. Make up games finding rhyming words. Teach young children to use the real telephone for calls that are meaningful to them, such as chats with friends and grandparents. Teach older children how to take phone messages.

Ask for feedback. Have your child rephrase and say back to you what he thinks you said.

7 Breeding a Reader

When my daughter was about 10 months old, I cashed in a gift certificate to a local bookstore. I bought children's classics. I bought pop-up books. I bought lift-the-flap books, talking books, and anything else I could carry. When I brought them home, she dived into the shopping bag. I was delighted. This kid was bound to be a reader! It wasn't long before I realized that her favorite book activity was building with them. She'd stack them, climb on them, make on- and off-ramps for her little cars with them. But she showed no interest, whatsoever, in being read to. Instead she'd climb off my lap with me in hot pursuit, still reading *The Cat in the Hat* to her disinterested ears. Eventually, a few years later, she did settle down to enjoy our daily reading, and it wasn't long before she clamored for more reading time than I could satisfy. But she had let me know from the start that she'd read on her terms, not mine.

For many kids, "reading" is both more and less what parents and teachers define as reading. One child may easily decode street signs but show little interest in literature. Another may crave read-aloud bedtime stories but pay scant attention to the decoding process and, in fact, resist any attempt to read by herself. A child may be far more interested in writing than in reading or be more focused on the pictures in a book than on the words. All of this is normal. As children begin the process of discovering what written words mean, the most important goal is that the experience be one of pleasant discovery.

Ready access to a variety of literature and information books is essential for that discovery to take place. Though many of the books that kids will need over the years can be borrowed from the library, each child also needs at least a few that are totally his own, a home library that inspires a child to grow beyond basic literacy and become a truly involved reader and idea communicator. Most importantly, he needs to see that *you* find reading to be a pleasurable, enlightening, engaging activity.

Reading Habits for Prereaders

Beyond reading to your child, read with him. Point to each word as you read, which allows him to see the spoken and written word connection. One study at the University of Illinois, which involved 650 kindergarteners, concluded that simply reading *to* children did little to teach them to read, whereas actively engaging them with the words *did* boost their skills. Point out similarities between words such as *cat* and *hat* or *cat* and *can*. As you touch each word with your finger, you're also helping your prereader get used to following words in a left-to-right pattern and a top-to-bottom page sequence. Point out and discuss the pictures on the page. Let him turn the pages so he can see that stories follow a predictable pattern, beginning on page one and working toward the end.

H e needs to see that *you* find reading to be a pleasurable, enlightening, engaging activity.

CHOOSING BOOKS FOR PREREADERS

For toddlers and preschoolers, the home library should contain their favorite storybooks, the ones they want to hear over and over again. Ask friends, teachers, and librarians to suggest appropriate books. Take him with you to the library or bookstore and watch to see what draws him in. Expand on his choices of the well-known character books that are likely to get his attention, such as Barney or Sesame Street offerings, and lead him also to the kids' classics, those books that have proven their worth over time. Include Mother Goose Rhymes, titles by Dr. Suess (*Green Eggs and Ham* and *Cat in the Hat*, for instance) and Margaret Wise Brown (especially *Goodnight Moon*). Go for variety, too, mixing in fact books with literature. Look for books of poetry, where the predictable rhyme enhances a child's understanding of letters and sounds. Likewise, stories with predictable sequences ("I'll huff and I'll puff and I'll blow your house down," from *The Three Little Pigs*, for example) alert kids to the look and sound of words and give them confidence in their abilities to master books as they guess words before you read them.

Find multiple opportunities for reading. While the bedtime story is a terrific ritual, it needn't be the only reading experience of the day. After nap time, when kids are alert, is another good reading opportunity. So is time spent waiting in line in the grocery store or as a wind-down after time at the playground. Also invite your child to read along with you as you go about your day—pointing out street signs, grocery items, mail—anything that contains the printed word. Point out the similarities between his name and other words. "Michael, your name starts with the same letter as the word *milk*," for instance. Keep it playful and don't push. Few children are ready to learn to decode a great many words before the age of 5 or 6.

Encourage written expression. Just as young artists delight in scribbling, young readers delight in forming their own letters and words. Help your child affix his own name (the first word that many children can read) onto his artwork, his bedroom door, and his toys. Use a variety of media to practice forming letters playfully: Trace letters in the sand, on paper, in a bowl of pudding, for instance. Write down the stories your child tells in his own special book. Keep a posted list of books you've read together.

Talk. The richer a child's language experience, the more ready he is to revel in the written word.

Reading Habits for Emergent Readers

Let your child set the pace. Most children learn to read between the ages of 5 1/2 and 8. The first thing parents of kids on the latter end of the spectrum need to do is RELAX. Don't let your anxiety become theirs. Early readers are not necessarily "brighter" than later readers, though the ways in which they learn to read can differ significantly. Kids who learn to read easily, who are able to see a word once and remember it, have internalized the connection between letter symbols and word sounds. Children who don't catch on effortlessly (which includes many kids) need more direct practice with phonics

The richer a child's language experience, the more ready he is to revel in the written word.

36

before they can make that connection. Kids are who truly struggling need not only *lots* of practice with phonics, but their parents' patience and support. Wherever your child is in her attempt to read, that's the point from which she must work. Showing your anxiety, displeasure or frustration won't help move her along any more quickly and will likely slow her down considerably.

Get extra help early if it's needed. If your child isn't moving toward literacy as quickly as you or her teachers think she should be, talk to her teachers and/or other professionals. You may find that she is, in fact, reading at a respectable level and you can adjust your expectations. Or you may find that intervention is called for. If necessary, have her tested. (If the school doesn't offer recommendations, call your local college, your pediatrician, or a social-service agency for a referral to a testing facility.) Have her hearing and vision checked since a problem with either can limit her access to understanding written and spoken language. Remember that having a learning "disability" usually points to a different learning style or a correctable physical problem and can be managed with the right help.

One-on-one help from a professional may be needed for a time. Don't put it off. Early intervention can prevent a child from getting into the habit of thinking she can't keep up. If she's having difficulty, let your child know that the problem isn't with her and that you and she and her teacher are all working together to make reading more pleasurable for her.

Most of the time, it's better to supply the difficult word and let the child move on with the story.

Help children enjoy their comfort zone. Oftentimes, once children have mastered easy-to-read picture books, parents foist harder books on them to keep the challenge high. While all kids do need challenges, they also need to spend some time in their own personal comfort zones. The 7-year-old who has just mastered reading *Goodnight Moon* on his own may enjoy reading that book again and again, to himself and aloud to anyone who will listen. Encourage it. Introduce chapter books and books with more words and fewer pictures during your regular time to read to him. He'll turn to these books on his own soon, but he needn't have to experience the struggle of reading these more difficult books before he's had a chance to enjoy reading the easier books fluently.

Keep frustration at bay. When an emergent reader is struggling with a word, it's tempting to tell her to "sound it out." Most of the time, it's better to supply the difficult word and let the child move on with the story. If a child chooses a book to read that is too challenging, suggest that you take turns reading pages. In that way, he gets the pleasure of having his reading choices respected without the unnecessary frustration of being unable to read at an enjoyable pace. While true literacy takes a few years to accomplish, let kids know that they are indeed reading, even though they can't read every word that comes their way.

Help them understand their frustrations. Some kids become very angry at books, at school, at you, and at themselves when they discover that merely wanting to read doesn't make them readers. Kids who are used to moving smoothly from home to preschool to the playground without struggling to learn something new and different can be surprised that the ability to read isn't automatically granted just for showing up at the school door. They get turned off to reading when they discover that it takes work to become a reader. My own struggling reader was mystified when she came to the word *enough* in a book she was scanning. "What's this word?" she asked. When I told her that e-n-o-u-g-h spelled *enough*, she threw the book down on the floor in frustration, saying, "if those letters spell *enough*, I give up!" The English language is not user-friendly as anyone learning to read it can attest. Frustrated readers need reminders that some of the most rewarding things they'll ever learn won't come easily but will come with practice.

Encourage multiple reading experiences. As with younger children, offer reading experiences wherever you are and with whatever materials grab your child's interest—at the store, on the back of a cereal box, when party invitations come in the mail. Don't hesitate to offer comic books or other "junk" reading. These high-interest materials may hold the key to the fluency a child needs. Invite your child to join you in reading a grown-up magazine or as you look through an atlas or cookbook or operations manual for your VCR. Have her review the travel brochures you've collected for your family's upcoming vacation. Let kids know that we all read for different reasons—for pleasure *and* to get information.

Provide tools and technology. Let children listen to audiotapes as they read along with the narrator. Or record yourself or your child reading a favorite book to play back as your child scans the written version of the story. Give early readers a ruler to use to follow words on the page, which many kids will find easier than pointing to each word as they read. Experiment to see what works best for your child.

Some of the most rewarding things they'll ever learn won't come easily but will come with practice.

Review the reading experience with readers. There's not a direct correlation between ease of decoding (sounding out) and ease of comprehension. Some fluent decoders can't recall what they've read or make reasonable predictions about what will happen next in a story. Some who struggle to sound out words have a good grasp of the story line. Both skills—decoding and comprehending—add up to literacy. Whether or not your child is decoding easily, ask appropriate questions to assure yourself and him that he's also reading for meaning.

Mix in writing with reading. Encourage kids to keep a reading journal, writing down the names of books they've read or heard. Have them write their own thank-you notes instead of writing them yourself or settling for verbal thank-yous only. Allow access to word processing and story-writing programs on the family computer. On vacation, have them write a few postcards of their own to their friends and relatives. Ask them to write their own wish lists for birthdays and holidays and their own party invitations and birthday cards to friends. Write notes to one another. Don't get too hung up on correct spelling for new readers and writers. While standardized spelling is essential for clear communication, it shouldn't be the focus for the first few years of literacy.

Reading Habits for Independent Readers

Read to them. Even kids who are reading on their own benefit enormously from having stories read to them because these can contain advanced vocabulary and intricate plots that they might not be able to handle on their own.

Celebrate reading. Consider giving your child a special book and magazine-buying allowance, separate from his regular allowance. When you come across a book or other reading material that supports a current interest, splurge on it. You'll not only promote his reading, but you'll let him know that you're paying attention to his interests.

Encourage reading for information. Parents naturally take great pleasure in seeing a child curled up with a good book. In addition to great literature, there's lots to be gained from reading informational materials. Reading maps, schedules, manuals, recipes, and tables of contents help children navigate the world and accomplish things on their own and add to their sense of competence.

BOOKS FOR EARLY READERS

As they grow, their general fiction and nonfiction collection needs to grow with them. Beyond these books, you'll need to add the reference books that every family needs: a dictionary and a thesaurus appropriate to the child's reading level, an atlas, and an encyclopedia. Even if you have an encyclopedia bundled into your computer, a bound-book version is extremely worthwhile. Also clip and pass along newspaper and magazine items you think your child would enjoy reading.

FINDING GOOD READING MATERIALS FOR KIDS

MAGAZINES

To find the right magazine for your child, review your library's copy of *Magazine for Kids and Teens,* published by EdPress and the International Reading Association. Or order your own copy by calling Edpress at Rowan College of New Jersey in Glassboro at (609) 256-4610. My recommendations include:

For preschoolers:

Ladybug (Carus Publications)
Sesame Street Magazine (Children's Television Workshop)

For school-age kids:

American Girl (Pleasant Company)
Crayola Kids (Meredith Corporation)
National Geographic World (National Geographic Society)
Puzzlemania (Highlights for Children)

BOOK RECOMMENDATIONS

A number of organizations publish annual lists of recommended books for children of different ages and interests.

- For the pamphlet, "Choosing a Child's Book," send a self-addressed, stamped envelop to The Children's Book Council, 568 Broadway, Suite 404. New York, NY 10012. Call them at (212) 966-1990 to find out what other current materials, such as wall posters, they may be able to send you.

- For a list of children's favorites called "Children's Choices," which are based on ages (5–8, 8–10, or 10–13), contact The International Reading Association at 800 Barksdale Road, Newark, DE 19714. For each list, include $1 and a self-addressed, stamped 9" × 12" envelope.
- For reviews of books and articles about reading, send for a sample of *The Horn Book,* 14 Beacon Street, Boston, MA 02108.
- For the pamphlet "Becoming a Nation of Readers: What Parents Can Do," send 50 cents to Consumer Information Center, Dept. 408Y, Pueblo, CO 81009.

For Parents:

Raising a Reader, by Paul Knapp (Main Street Books)
RIF Guide to Encouraging Young Readers (Smithsonian Institution)
Choosing Books for Children, by Betsy Hearne (Delacorte)
A Parent's Guide to Children's Reading, by Nancy Larrick (Pocket Books)
For Reading Out Loud, by Margaret Kimmel and Elizabeth Segel (Dell/Delacorte)
The New Read-Aloud Handbook, by Jim Trelease (Penguin)
Choosing Books for Kids, by Joanne Oppenheim et al. (Bank Street)
Getting Ready to Read, by Betty Boegehold (Bank Street)

8 Tools for Learning

Imagine showing up at work and finding all of the normal tools of operation missing—no computers, no desks, not even a blunt-end pencil. You've found the perfect excuse to spend the day doing anything but your job. When a child's home is bereft of the basic machinery of learning, she, too, is free to do nothing. (On occasion, of course, doing nothing is a good thing; see #14.) If instead, the child's home is filled with the tools of learning—the reading and research resources, the art supplies, the jump ropes, the board games, the bikes, and the houseplants—then she has at her fingertips the things she needs to build her brain.

Much of what kids need in terms of physical tools is in place in most homes. Any stuff that kids can observe and handle is educational, including the dust under the beds. A colander, bucket, and bathtub give kids lots of opportunities to learn about the qualities of water and the differences between solid containers and ones with holes. A large empty box is a perfect carrying case, spaceship, puppet theater, or whatever your child can imagine it to be.

Beyond the found objects of learning and the freedom to explore those items and the everyday experiences you provide, however, kids also benefit from having certain decidedly "educational" tools at their disposal. The items need not cost a bundle. But they need to belong to the child in that he's allowed to use them freely. Here's a breakdown of the essential brain-building equipment to buy, rent, borrow, or build:

A personal work station. From the time they're toddlers until they're off to college, learners need a place to put their most essential stuff. A work station should consist of a table or desk, containers for storing needed supplies, shelving to store reading and other materials, a comfortable chair, and good lighting. Each child needs his or her own space, where projects can be left undisturbed by others. It's fine to do homework at the kitchen table if your child prefers to be in the middle of the action while working, but she also needs a place that is hers where she can retreat and where she can organize and store her work.

Building and art supplies. Pencils, pens, crayons, chalk, lots of paper, glue, scissors, tape, pipe cleaners, stickers, straws, clay, blocks, paints, and paint brushes—kids need these materials, as well as hammers, nails, cloth, wood, yarn, and whatever other unstructured materials they can get their hands on to formulate ideas and to express those ideas in concrete, touchable ways. Kits and building supplies are great for school-age kids who take pride in re-creating useful items. Though your family may have a computer program that allows for all sorts of creative endeavors, kids also need handleable, bendable, breakable (and, therefore, fixable) materials with which to work.

Any stuff that kids can observe and handle is educational, including the dust under the beds.

Games and toys. Toys and games are not frills. Board games, decks of cards, costumes, action figures and dolls, and puzzles all help kids learn essential social and intellectual skills. Through play with these defined, more structured materials, children learn role-playing, language skills, math concepts, and living skills. Toys and games are not just the province of very young children. Older kids, teens, and adults all benefit from playing.

Sports equipment. Tricycles, bicycles, balls, jump ropes, and skates not only help children to develop their muscles and spatial skills but also provide the perfect means of developing the competence to meet mental challenges. For many children, there's a strong correlation between developing motor skills and developing language and logic skills. Physical activity also encourages healthy body-building and stress-reducing habits.

Useful technology. Calculators are not a substitute for learning to add, but they're great tools for checking your work. Computers have become a common tool in most classrooms and homes. Kids above the second grade or so who don't have regular access to an up-to-date model, including a good word processing program, will find themselves less able than their peers to develop computer writing skills and enhance the presentation of their work.

9 Using Computers at Home

Computers have no value other than what they can help the person using them do.

Being wired doesn't mean what it used to. The term once implied a kind of high-strung personality, but now it means simply that a person is plugged into the latest technology.

As dazzling as the new technology can appear to be, it's important that parents, teachers, and kids see computers for what they are: machines, useful tools, that can help get a job done. They have no value other than what they can help the person using them do. Perhaps because of their relative newness in the business of learning or simply because of their high price, computers in schools are both underutilized and are given a glorified status that leads everyone to believe that they can solve problems just by being there. In many schools, particularly where classroom computers are in short supply, there are the so-called "computer labs," in which children are taught how to make the machine work. This would be the equivalent of having "pencil labs" back in the late 1800s, to help kids make the switch from writing with chalk on slates to using pencil on paper. It's a bit ridiculous. When used primarily to see how they work or simply for drill and practice, computers are costly alternatives to already-available methods of learning.

It's in their higher functions—the ability to branch out, to "read" the skill level of the learner and to adjust the pace and scope of learning accordingly, and to link users around the globe to each other and to all of the world's information—that computers prove their worth.

One study, done by Susan Haugland, Ph.D., a child-development expert at Southeast Missouri State University, found that certain educational software programs can actually increase children's IQs by an average of six points. Before rushing out to buy the biggest and best computer that money can buy and stocking up on software, however, note that her study also showed that using uninspiring programs, particularly those designed for drill and practice, can blunt a child's creativity and actually slow learning. The key, clearly, is choosing software wisely and using it well.

Before purchasing any program, talk with other users about their favorites; talk, especially to teachers who use computers in their classrooms, but be wary of anyone who boasts about programs that are heavy on drill and practice. It's cheaper to go with printed workbooks than to invest in this kind of software. A good program, like any good teacher, encourages the learner to pursue knowledge and doesn't just test for it. Programs that "branch," allowing students to seek and find and create ideas in ever-more challenging ways and that encourage exploration do the job best.

To find these programs, read software reviews in computer and family magazines. If possible, try out a program before you buy it. If a seller isn't able to let you try out the software in the store, be sure it offers a risk-free return policy for programs that don't live up to their fancy packaging. Get familiar with the leaders in the field of developing

The key is choosing software wisely and using it well.

47

software for kids, such as Broderbund, Edmark, The Learning Company, and Maxis. Many Disney, Apple Home Learning, IBM, and Sierra On-Line programs are also excellent. Check out your library or child's school for a copy of *Children's Software Revue,* a bi-monthly newsletter, which details the plusses and minuses of various software. (To subscribe or request a sample, call 800-993-9499.) To take a look at kids' software before buying, you can also subscribe to *Kidsoft*, which provides CD-ROM samples of programs. Call Kidsoft at 800-354-6150.

The bottom line. Can your child get by without a computer? Yes. But, increasingly, a wider and wider gulf will form between him and his wired peers who are technically savvy. However, simply having a computer and the peripheral equipment confers no benefits if they are not used wisely. Used improperly, for example, playing hours and hours of mindless games, the machines can do more harm than good. So could the microwave, of course, if it isn't used correctly.

GREAT PROGRAMS TO GET YOU STARTED

The following is a short list of programs that are already considered classics. The prominent skill area is shown, though most of these good programs help kids develop a variety of skills.

FOR AGES 4 TO 9

Reader Rabbit 1, 2, and 3 (The Learning Company) reading
Wiggleworks (Apple Home Learning) writing
Kid Works Deluxe (Davidson) writing
Millie's Math House (Edmark) math
Thinking Things 1 and 2 (Edmark) logic
Gus Goes to Cyberopolis (Modern Media Ventures)
    imagination, creativity
Aladdin Activity Center (Disney) imagination, creativity
Jumpstart Toddlers, Kindergarten, First Grade, Second Grade
    (Knowledge Adventure) general knowledge

FOR AGES 7 TO 12

Storybook Maker (Jostens Home Learning) writing
Creative Writer (Edmark) writing
Storybook Weaver (MECC) writing
The Amazing Writing Machine (Broderbund) writing
Math Workshop (Broderbund) math
Imagination Express/Destination Castle/Destination
    Rainforest, etc. (Edmark) imagination, creativity
Sim Town/Sim City, etc. (Maxis) imagination, creativity, logic
The Magic Schoolbus Series (Scholastic) science
Thinking Things 3 (Edmark) logic
Logical Journey (Broderbund) logic
Elroy Hits the Pavement (Headbone Interactive) logic

FOR FAMILIES

If the computer will be used by a variety of family members, consider installing a program such as *At Ease,* to block access to your files from other users. Also, get a good word processing program, such as *Microsoft Word 5.1* or higher, which is far more versatile than the word processing program that comes bundled with your machine. For those who are at the hunt-and-peck stage of keyboarding, try *Mario Teaches Typing.* Be aware that antivirus programs, such as *Norton Utilities,* may not be compatible with a number of children's programs. (Also note that you don't need an antivirus program unless you're on-line or trade software with others.) Encyclopedia are often bundled in with your computer. They have advantages over book versions in that they certainly take up less space, are less costly than a traditional 26-volume set, and are easily upgradable. They are far more cumbersome, however, for most quick-reference projects than are books.

10 Signing on to the Net

The first time I signed on to my on-line service, I felt like I finally entered the modern world. Like any time traveler, I was both nervous and enthralled by the possibilities. I made up an on-line address (MKKIDSMART@AOL.com) and, over the next few weeks, logged up a few hundred hours scanning the service's offerings. I learned to navigate the chat rooms, and met dozens of teachers, parents, and others who provided many helpful ideas and leads to help me research this and other works. Some of the best advice pointed me toward good, old-fashioned books. That didn't surprise me.

Some other "information" was useless, and I was reminded that information, even when it arrives in a fancy, electronic package, is only as good as its source and that on-line sources need to be scrutinized as much as any others. I "met" one chat-room devotee, who wrote in capital letters (the on-line equivalent of shouting) that the only thing wrong with American education today was that teachers were no longer free to beat their students. I ignored him and eventually he went away, though not before depositing over 100 messages in my e-mail box.

Then I got my first bill, and that was really a surprise. Immediately, I put myself on a strict on-line allowance. There, in a nutshell, is the upside and the downside of this technology. If you're interested in signing up and logging on:

Going On-Line

There are two ways to go on-line. One is to sign up with an on-line service, such as America Online, CompuServe, or Prodigy. All services include access to the Internet, a vast network of connected computers, and the World Wide Web, a large part of the Internet that offers a collection of sites to "visit." The other means is to hook up with a local access provider, which will link you to the Internet. By mid-1996, more than 9.5 million American households were connected. About 50 percent of America's schools (but just about 3 percent of individual classrooms) were on-line, and the federal government had set a goal of having all schools wired by the year 2000.

Is going on-line something you need to do for your child's education? No, at least not immediately for most kids. Most grade-schoolers who aren't heavily into research can work well without going on-line, just as they can work well without having a library of thousands of books right now. On the other hand, a child in high school who spends lots of time in the library researching can work from home and have more information at his or her fingertips than any single library could possibly provide.

If your family has far-flung relatives or friends (who are also on-line) and you'd like more opportunity to "talk" in real time without the cost of long-distance phone calls, you'll like e-mail. And if you and your kids have a need to get the latest information on any topic or just want to talk with others around the world about mutual interests, you will find ample opportunity here. There are, however, some potential drawbacks.

Keeping It Kid-Friendly

Like other media, a child's on-line time needs to be monitored to protect him from images and people that can harm him.

No doubt you've heard horror stories about kids getting swept up in seedy sidestreets of the net. Though it's not as common as the headlines suggest, a single incident of a child conversing with an on-line creep is enough to discourage many parents from allowing any access. Like television and other media, a child's on-line time needs to be monitored to protect him from images and from people that can harm him.

On-line services try to keep inappropriate material out of the kids' on-line mailboxes by offering "kids only" areas that are screened. America Online lets parents close off e-mail, chat rooms, and discussion groups where monitoring isn't possible. CompuServe offers WOW!, designed especially for kids, which offers family-friendly content. Additionally, its costs are set to under $20 per month for unlimited on-line time, whereas hefty bills can run up if a family logs on frequently through other services. There are various programs on the market that, while no substitute for parental involvement, also severely limit kids' possible missteps. Red flags that can alert you to your child's inappropriate access include secretive or excessive computer use and phone bills that include long-distance phone numbers unfamiliar to you. This could indicate that your child is contacting an on-line connection by telephone.

Parents can also purchase screening software (see box). Finally, the Recreational Software Advisory Council offers Internet site creators the option of rating their own sites on a scale of 0 to 4 so that browsers, those looking over the Internet's lists of possible sites to visit, can steer their kids to the sites deemed acceptable according to the rating. Those who have *Cyber Patrol* or *Explorer* (3.0 version) installed will benefit from automatic blocking of restricted sites and/or unrated sites.

It's not just the content found on the net that can cause problems for some users. Some kids (and adults, too) get carried away with their life on-line and spend far too much time hooked up in a form of faceless communication that stunts real interaction. The anonymity afforded on-line users sometimes leads them to shed inhibitions and get involved in behaviors that they'd never consider in face-to-face communication.

Know the rules of the road. Kids who are on-line need to know the rules of the road. The National Center for Missing and Exploited Children, proposes these on-line rules for kids:

- I will not give out personal information such as my address, phone number, or the name and location of my school without my parents' permission.
- I will tell my parents right away if I come across any information that makes me feel uncomfortable.
- I will never agree to get together with someone I meet on-line without checking with my parents. If my parents agree to a meeting, I will make sure that it is in a public place and bring my mother or father along.

- I will never send a person my picture or anything else without checking with my parents.
- I will not respond to any messages that are mean or in any way make me feel uncomfortable. It is not my fault if I get such a message. If I do, I will tell my parents right away so that they can contact the on-line service.
- I will talk with my parents so that we can set up rules for going on-line. We will decide on the time of day that I can be on-line, the length of time that I can be on-line, and appropriate areas for me to visit.

SITES TO VISIT

Here are some on-line destinations worth visiting:

http://parentsoup.com—offers a compendium of useful parenting information.

http://www.psych.med.umich.edu/web/aacap/factsFam—presents fact sheets prepared by the American Academy of Child and Adolescent Psychiatry on forty-six topics related to child and adolescent psychology.

http://ericps.ed.uluc.edu/npin/parenting.html—connects you to ERIC (Educational Resources Information Center) archives, designed to help parents and teachers access information on education and other topics.

http://family.com—leads browsers to family-friendly sites as well as school-related information and shopping sources.

BOOKS TO GUIDE NET USE

Kidnet: The Kid's Guide to Surfing Through Cyberspace, by Debra and Brad Schepps (HarperCollins)

Student's Guide to the Internet, by David Clark (alpha books)

Parental Control Software

Cybersitter

Surfwatch

Net Nanny

Microsoft's Explorer

Cyber Patrol (which is provided to CompuServe and Prodigy users).

11 Putting TV in its Place

About three years ago, a granola-fed, 100 percent cotton-clad little boy, a playground pal of my then 4-year-old, came to visit. I was on deadline and wanted the kids to play quietly while I worked, but it was not to be. They fought over the Duplo blocks. They fought over the cowboy/cowgirl hat. She fell down. He claimed he hadn't pushed her. Exasperated, I suggested that they sit quietly on the sofa and watch a *Barney* tape.

I might as well have suggested that they eat poisoned popcorn in a burning room. Our young visitor screamed in horror, "Television is bad, bad, bad! I can't watch it! I won't watch it! I'll tell my mother on you! You can't make me watch it!" He hid behind the sofa as I cajoled him out with promises of unsweetened yogurt and a cross-my-heart swear not to turn on the TV until he was safely home. When his father arrived to take him home, I recalled the incident. He patted the boy on his fashionable head and said, "Good for you!" I was glad to see them leave.

There's no doubt in parents' and educators' minds that too much TV is not a good thing. We all agree, too, that bad TV, even in limited doses, is still bad TV. But most of us, unlike our guest, have allowed television to be part of our lives. The good news is that good TV is an incredible source of knowledge, inspiration, and fun. Kids who watch no TV can be socially limited, unable to discuss popular programs with their peers. Moreover, they miss some great stuff. Studies show that preschoolers who watch about an hour a day of educational programs such as *Sesame Street* surpass their non-TV-watching peers in both academic and social learning.

Kids who watch too much television, however, suffer the greater loss. They have limited time to pursue other, more active and engaging activities and are likely to be exposed to inappropriate ideas and images.

According to *American Demographics,* preschoolers watch the most TV—about 26 hours a week. That drops to just 5 to 6 hours a week, on average, for teens. So clearly, kids themselves tend to find better things to do once they're old enough to decide how to spend their time. In the meantime, however, children's television viewing is more than a passive waste of time for many, many kids. According to the American Academy of Pediatrics committee on communication, television:

- desensitizes kids to violence
- leads to obesity
- relaxes kids' avoidance of premature sexual activity, alcohol, and drug use.

The committee notes that American teens see an estimated 14,000 sexual references per year on TV, though only about 150 of these make any reference to sexual responsibility, abstinence, or contraception. The daytime talk shows, particularly, can

*I*f they're not watching TV, they can't be expected to watch the walls.

READ MORE ABOUT IT

For ideas on TV alternatives, here are some of the best books on the subject:

For Parents of Preschoolers:

Child's Play, by Leslie Hamilton (Crown)

365 TV-Free Activities You Can Do with Your Child, by Steve and Ruth Bennett (Bob Adams, Inc.)

365 Days of Creative Play, by Sheila Ellison and Judith Gray, publisher TK

continued on next page

give children a very skewed view of the world as the hosts parade the most dysfunctional souls in the country across the screen. Kids, with their limited experience and pseudosophistication easily begin to believe that what they see is normal. Relatively innocuous sitcoms, dramas, and cartoons, in excess, dull children's senses. The evening news can be terrifying for a young child. Even too much educational TV is too much TV. Before tossing it out or limiting it too much, however, consider these strategies:

Move it. Put the set in an inconvenient place, not in your child's room or in the middle of the living room. If they've got to retrieve it from the hallway in order to watch it, kids will think twice before going to the trouble.

Let kids know what you do and don't expect in terms of viewing. It's not fair to let children guess about what's allowable and what's not. Tell them how much of what programs you permit. If you've decided to cut down on television, be clear about the new house rules. Expect a period of withdrawal if you're switching from a laissez-faire attitude to a weekend-only policy. Be sensitive to kids' anxiety and be available to involve them in some other, more active pursuit.

Use available technology. Monitoring what your children watch all day is not always possible. Take advantage of technology, in the form of the new V-chip and other parental blocking devices (such as Parental Control, Channel Block, or Child Lock) that have been built into many televisions manufactured since 1993. These older blockers allow you to limit the amount of viewing time or to block access to specific stations and are programmed through your remote control. Some, however, can be overridden simply by pulling the plug on the TV and replugging it, a system most kids are likely to figure out.

Watch a program, not TV. Don't put the TV on mindlessly "to see what's on." Know beforehand if there's a program worth your kids' time and only turn on the TV for that show. Once a week, when the TV booklet arrives, review the schedule to see what's worth tuning in for. Look particularly for recommendations for children's programs, included in many guides.

Don't make TV too big of a deal. Don't use TV as the bargaining chip for every behavior you want or don't want. As one child told me, "I can trade a TV show for almost anything. Like I beg to watch something like *Walker* that my mom doesn't like and even though I don't like it either she'll say, 'How about a new book if you don't watch that.' Or if I do something she doesn't like she'll say, 'Okay, no TV tonight.' She thinks I care about it much more than I do."

Set up a "pay-TV" system of your own. A number of parents report that their kids are willing to forgo TV for a reward. This system, however, has a more positive spin to it: "I give each of my kids two dollars in quarters on Sunday night," says one mom of three. "They have to pay me 25 cents for each half-hour of television." She reports that each has gone from spending his or her money by Tuesday, to getting through the whole week, to saving toward other things. "My oldest son," she boasts, "has gone from being

---

For Grade-Schoolers:

Fun Station: Exploring Nature, by Brenda Walpole

The Happy Camper Handbook, by Michael Elsohn Ross

The Kids' Summer Handbook, by Jane Drake and Ann Love

The American Boy's Handy Book, by Daniel Beard

a TV junkie to almost eliminating television from his life. In just a few months, he saved up $30 toward the cost of the roller blades he desperately wanted."

Offer alternative activities. If they're not watching TV, they can't be expected to watch the walls. Make sure that they have the materials they need on hand to do projects. Give them lots of opportunity to be outdoors involved in a physical activity. Make your home available to their friends, which lessens the desire to head to their friends' homes for some television viewing.

Be matter-of-fact about your rules. A simple, "Not on a school night" or "Your half an hour is up" is more effective than arguing and giving in.

Limit eating and watching. Most TV watching is passive. Add to that a big bowl of ice cream and you've got the makings of an obese, physically unfit child. Limit TV snacking so that the association of nibbling and viewing isn't ingrained.

Play fair. Don't sequester yourself in the TV room while banning the kids.

Watch programs together. Television, even when it's not at its best, offers great opportunities to discuss some more important issues. And watching something great together is simply great fun.

12 Monitoring the Culture

Some of us claim to be liberals and are willing to call any form of self-expression "art." Some of us label ourselves as conservatives who firmly believe in the moral necessity of a free-market system that produces all the junk our culture offers. Most of us, of course, huddle and muddle together in the middle, both caught up in the culture and appalled by aspects of it. What sort of gatekeeping works? Some ideas:

Minimize materialism. Try not to make shopping the main weekend outing for the family. Shop with a list of things you need rather than browse for things you neither need nor thought you wanted until you happened to see them. When kids clamor for things advertised on TV, help them see how the advertisers are trying to manipulate them into buying something that may not be as cool as it looks. The action-figure army helicopter, for instance, doesn't really fly as it's shown to on the ad. (Responding to ads is perhaps the one instance where children *should* be taught cynicism.) It's important to be sensitive to kids' needs to have some of the things their friends have. It's equally important, however, to draw the line where you see fit.

Kids need exposure to positive aspects of the culture as much as they need guidance to reject the garbage.

View movies, computer games, and TV programs together. If you're not sure if a certain offering is right for your child, check it out with her. "If you want to see that movie, I'll take you." This will give you the opportunity to discuss any aspects with her that you may find worthy of your input. It will also give your child entry into the same cultural world as her peers, but with a navigator. One friend who had banned *The Simpsons* was surprised to find how value-laden the program was in spite of its reputation for crassness and pursuit of underachievement. Her flexibility in changing her rules gave her son an increased respect for her judgment. "He actually agreed with me when I still said no to 'Mortal Kombat,' " she reports.

Don't give up. Certainly, enjoying popular culture together gets more difficult as kids mature. At some point, though parents still need to make their views known, they need to cede the responsibility of choice to their children. That's where a lifetime of mutual respect can pay off. As one mom of a 15-year-old says, "I told my son that the music he was enjoying—with lyrics about hate of women and love of violence—was an affront to everything I knew about his beliefs. He claimed it 'was just music.' I said that it glorified ideas that were repugnant, that it fostered disrespect of me, his mother, by boys and men everywhere. I added that his liking it reduced my respect for him. To my great relief, he saw my point. He found alternative music to enjoy, still some things I wasn't crazy about but at least not vulgar." An outcome like this is possible only when kids know that they share responsibility for the culture and when their views and parents' views are both given respect.

Enjoy the positive. Kids need exposure to positive aspects of the culture as much as they need guidance to reject the garbage. Provide ample opportunities for them to sample quality. After all, quality media will only be produced if there's an audience for it.

13 Encouraging Special interests

The world may not need a few million paleontologists, but that shouldn't preclude encouraging a child to know all there is to know about dinosaurs. In other words, a child's passionate interest in a subject needn't be practical. It doesn't have to relate in any direct way to schoolwork. It doesn't have to be career-oriented. The fact is that *any* interest supports a child's determination to know more and that, in itself, is a good thing. A deep interest and knowledge of a subject can be a very self-affirming experience. As one 9-year-old said, "because I love wild animals, especially panthers, leopards, and other big cats, I know for sure that I am me and not my brother or anybody else."

Developing a special interest or a hobby is more than a nice way to spend an afternoon. A hobby can inspire new ways of thinking. It can provide a release from stress. It can feed a child's ego by serving up a healthy portion of competence. There are many ways to help support and build your child's interests:

Respect her choices. Even if you could care less about car engines, your child's interest in V-6s can take her far. Unless there is an overriding moral or safety reason to nix an interest, get behind your child and help her pursue her passion. Show your support of an interest by helping a child earn the money or otherwise acquire the stuff she needs to learn and do more.

*I*nstead of letting children help you, take on the role of helper yourself only if asked and stay out of the way if not asked.

Don't take over. Too much involvement on your part can sap the joy out of your child's interest. The kid who wants to build a treehouse may, indeed, build a "better" one with you, giving instructions and saving him from time-consuming "mistakes." But then, whose house will it be?

Help build collections. Find occasions to give your child additions to his collections. If your child loves drawing and making crafts, collect usable debris from your office—Styrofoam peanuts, bent paper clips, etc.—to bring home, for example.

Enlarge the scope of her interest. Take your young aviator to an air-and-space museum; visit a working steam-engine line when vacationing with your model train builder. Take your doll collector to a doll hospital. Take behind-the-scenes tours of your local bakery, firehouse—anyplace that intrigues your child.

Help develop a new interest. If you have a hobby, invite your child to join you. For those kids who seem content to try nothing new, sign them up for lessons or clubs that may spark an interest.

Expose your child to the larger world. Only a child who has seen and heard a harmonica will be inspired to learn to play one. Only a child who has tried to snowplow can develop an interest in skiing. Giving kids lots of opportunities to sample the world's possibilities whets their appetites for more.

Find related materials. Your child may have a few hundred items in a collection. What other things might help her pursue her interest along slightly divergent paths? The child who collects model cars can join a hobby club, can build a display case, can rent films on the subject, and can become a pen pal with someone who shares that interest.

RESOURCES

- **The Encyclopedia of Associations.** This thick volume, available in most libraries, can put you and your child in touch with professionals—and lots of free samples and literature—from almost any field. A kid with an interest in model trains can get in touch with model and steam train associations, photography associations (for photos of trains), etc.
- **Manufacturers.** Write to product manufacturers of products that relate to your child's area of interest. One high-school-age rain-forest researcher I know was able to receive various raw product samples of rain-forest products—gum, rubber, bark, etc.—for use in her school project.
- **Researchers.** Check out the Internet or local colleges and universities for researchers working on a topic that interests your child. One 12-year-old budding botanist entered into a regular on-line communication with a college botany professor, who supplies him with hybridizing experiments to work on. (Of course, his parents monitor the communication.)

---

14 Allowing Boredom

Early on, I learned never to say, "Mom, I'm bored" because she usually found something distasteful, like room cleaning, for me to do to wile away my time. I've passed that noble tradition on to my own daughter, who would rather dance on hot coals than pick up a stray sock. As a result she rarely claims to be bored.

Young children in any normally bustling environment are never bored. A toddler can spend long periods of time happily moving from building and dismantling a stack of pots, to crawling in and out of a large box, to developing new and improved recipes for mud pies. Curiosity is a young child's constant playmate and as long as her curiosity isn't unduly thwarted by too much emphasis on neatness or safety, her mind and her whole being are engaged.

Many older children have been conditioned to be entertained and react to the lack of entertainment as boredom. Children who've overlearned caution, who must refrain from making a mess, who've been offered your quick attention or the consolation prize of a television program before any noticeable boredom can settle in, and who have limited materials at their disposal *can* become bored. But boredom is not a lack of activity. It's a lack of engagement in what is available to spur the mind and move the body.

Parents can't protect kids from boredom. Nor should we try. Given a chance to take root, boredom makes itself disappear as long as no one tries to rescue a child from it. In fact, when a family's hectic schedule seems to preclude boredom, it's essential that parents make time to ensure that the kids get to experience some boredom. Only when there's "nothing to do" can kids invent something new, discover a new use for a familiar object, or dream of a place that only they can see.

These habits can help your child use boredom well:

Schedule down time. Make sure that some part of the day is regularly free from scheduling—no homework, no lessons, no electronic distractions—just a kid and some stuff and the time to play.

Don't overreact to a lack of activity. Lying on a bed and staring at the ceiling may look to you like wasting time. To a child, it may involve fantasy play, deep thinking, planning, and a host of other active-mind activities.

Model mind meanderings. What do the shapes of the clouds remind you of? What do the same shapes make your child think about? Make the time to share your musings, giving your child a model for using the landscape around them imaginatively.

Provide free-form play materials. Keep a box of interesting stuff around—a broken clock, old magazines—for your child to explore and experiment with.

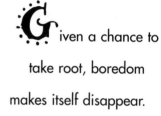

iven a chance to take root, boredom makes itself disappear.

Kids who can follow their own pace are better able to learn to satisfy their curiosity.

Adjust your pace. It's tempting to hurry kids through the day, asking them to keep up with your tempo. But kids who can follow their own pace as they go about your day are better able to learn to satisfy their curiosity. Thus, when faced with a blank schedule, they are armed with the tools to look more closely at the world around them. A child who is allowed to dawdle on your walk home, taking the time to study the cracks in the sidewalk, is better prepared to find things of interest wherever she may be.

Suggest good deeds. When kids are not bored, make a list of people or organizations in your community or big jobs around their home that could use their help. Post it. When there's more down time than a child knows what to do with, suggest that they turn to the list. Be careful not to make this a punitive response to a child's claim of boredom but simply a good use of their time.

15 Getting Physical

A quick test: Define the word *lap*:

    a) the place made when you sit

    b) the distance around the track or across the swimming pool.

Even if you aren't training for the next marathon, you can help your child to really be "on his toes." Here's how:

Eat right. Kids need to eat right, and the earlier they begin good eating habits, the better. Helping them understand that food is fuel for energy and growth is key since all children regard being strong and big as assets. You don't want to get into the business of policing their every bite or asking them to join "the clean plate club." On the contrary, focusing on food usually backfires. Instead you simply need to provide a range of healthful foods while limiting (but not eliminating) their access to junk. Also, never send a child to school without a good breakfast. A hungry child, by about 10 a.m., tunes out anything but the sound of his rumbling stomach. Good morning choices include any combination of complex carbohydrates and simple sugars (breads, cereals, and fruits, for example) and proteins (meat, eggs, nuts, beans) and some dairy (milk, cheese, yogurt).

Get enough sleep. The vast majority of American kids—and their parents—are sleep deprived. Though most school-age kids and teens need between 10 and 11 hours of sleep a day, most get by on 8 or 9 hours or even less. The accumulated sleep loss results in behavioral problems and attention-deficit problems that can better be cured by more sack time than by punitive responses to misbehavior or through drugs or therapy. Too little sleep also inhibits the brain's ability to remember things learned during wakefulness.

A number of studies, including one of human sleep and memory undertaken at the Weizmann Institute of Science in Israel, conclude that during the deepest stage of sleep subjects reorganized information they had collected during their workdays into memorable and retrievable chunks. Those whose sleep was interrupted were less apt to remember lessons of the day before. High schoolers, particularly, do better in school when they can enjoy a good night's sleep, yet many are in early-riser programs and are busy with after-school clubs and work so that they are constantly battling fatigue. According to research conducted at the Sleep Disorder Center of Johns Hopkins University, students who started classes at 9:30 a.m. fared significantly better in school than those who started at the more traditional time of 7:30 a.m. Yet few schools offer the option of a later start time. That leaves an earlier bedtime (with perhaps fewer after-school jobs and other commitments) as the best option for most children.

To see if your child is getting all the sleep she needs is quite simple: If she awakens on her own each morning before school, the chances are that she's getting enough sleep. If, however, she relies on you or an alarm clock to rouse her into a disgruntled wakefulness, she needs more zzzz's.

Exercise. For many kids, physical learning and physical activity are overtaken by an emphasis on desk-bound academic achievement once school begins. Often the switch is abrupt, causing disequilibrium, which often looks like hyperactivity. A recent kindergarten grad who suddenly has to sit still in a first-grade classroom for much of her day is going to feel (and act) out of sorts if she's not given plenty of opportunity to use her body, to move, to play physically.

But if she has the opportunity to exercise regularly, she has an outlet. She also can modify any stress that the new expectations for learning place on her. Many children also learn academic subjects—particularly math—better when they can move during the lessons, clapping out the times tables, for instance.

If physical activity is limited during your child's school day, work with the school to increase the daily activity level. Also offer plenty of after-school opportunities to run, jump, ride a bike, and more. Offer to join a child during a hike to help her review spelling words or memorize a sonnet instead of having her practice at the dining table. You'll both feel better, and she'll learn more. Support her interest in soccer as much as you support her interest in reading. Both will serve her well. Aim for a minimum of 15 minutes of nonstop, strenuous, aerobic exercise a day (biking, jumping rope, skating, swimming, for

If she awakens on her own each morning, the chances are that she's getting enough sleep.

71

example) or 30 minutes of more moderate exercise (moderate-to-brisk walking, playground activity, etc.). Also, help your child focus on what her body can do, not simply on her appearance.

Adjust the lighting. Artificial lighting has an enormous effect on humans and too much or too little of it at the wrong times can play havoc with the brain's ability to function at its peak. In one study conducted at Brigham and Women's Hospital in Boston, researchers found that too much indoor light in the evening can delay a person's ability to fall asleep when he needs to and can result in his being tired even after getting the number of hours of rest he needs. Too little light during winter daytimes—usually the result of having incandescent bulbs instead of full-spectrum ones during indoor activities—can result in depression. As much as possible, let the indoor lighting situation mimic nature's own. Replace ordinary bulbs and fluorescent lighting in your child's learning environment with full-spectrum bulbs, and encourage your child's school to do the same.

Help your child focus on what her body can do, not simply on her appearance.

72

16 Reducing Stress

i recently went to one of those huge office-supply places to buy a refill for my address book, I was struck by a display of Mickey Mouse-adorned date books, and others with pictures of rock stars. Cool, I thought. Now an executive can maintain a sense of whimsy and opt for one of these trendy-looking books over the staid leather variety. A salesman seeing me look them over offered, "Those are really hot with the kids. We can't keep them in stock." I shouldn't have been surprised. The frenetic schedules of many 10-year-olds could put a CEO to shame. Kids, like adults, need ways to keep track of their many, many activities and appointments. But datebooks for kids? I felt sorry for any child whose schedule was complicated enough to need one. So I bought one for myself, with a picture of Minnie Mouse in a red polka-dot dress.

While some stress is good—a deadline that promises closure and the hard work that goes into meeting a goal, for instance, but a lot simply robs us of joy. Here are some ways to cut down on it.

Drop unnecessary commitments. No matter how appealing some after-school activities might be, if your child is overscheduled, suggest that he pick one or two activities that he really wants to pursue and let the others drop for now.

*T*he frenetic

schedules of many

10-year-olds could put a

CEO to shame.

Focus on the present. In an attempt to prepare for the future or to cram in all we can into this afternoon, we can sometimes forget the pleasure that a *slow* walk-through now can bring. There's really no need to hurry through each and every day. To a child, a few hours spent watching the ducks on a pond is more meaningful and memorable than rushing through that experience so that no one misses out on the "fun" of also flying the kite you packed for the outing playing with the Frisbee, and getting in a round of miniature golf. Those other activities can be saved for another day. Letting your child set the pace can result in a much calmer, more pleasantly focused day.

Take a break from routine. Go so far as to play hooky with your kids. A break from performing can be good for everyone's perspective and energy level.

Don't try to make kids happy too much. While we needn't set out to make them miserable either, trying too hard too often to ensure that they're happy will always make them (and us) tense. A child who needs to be fed a constant diet of good feelings, praise, and gifts is going to be anxious because he'll be forever striving for one more little token of our affection. True happiness can only come with satisfaction, and the gotta-be-happy kid is rarely satisfied.

Respect fears and anxieties. We all have some anxieties and worries. As adults, we're usually able to rationalize our way out of total phobia and debilitating fears. But 4-year-olds, with their limited experience, really do believe there are monsters in the closet. Ten-year-olds worry fiercely about their parents' well-being. And teens can honestly feel they will die if they're rejected by friends or the school of their dreams. Children who are afraid of something—no matter how irrational it may seem to us—need to have their feelings respected. They can't be dismissed with a "That's ridiculous" or a "Grow up." Respecting their feelings involves letting them talk about what troubles them and helping them develop strategies for coping. It means not forcing them to feel differently than they do.

Limit kids' exposure to grown-up anxieties. Openness in a family is generally a good thing, but parents can go overboard sharing their lives—and their worries—with their kids. If you lose your job, it's okay to let your children know that the family may have to cut down on expenses for a time. But kids should not be privy to your fears about foreclosure. Instead, they need to know that you're working to solve whatever problems may arise. They also need to be told that they are not responsible for you and that their needs don't present a burden to you.

Be a confident and relatively consistent parent. Children who lack reasonable rules and consistent routines in their lives are always looking for the boundaries. When parents set safe limits, kids feel protected.

17 Teaching Life Skills

Minutes after having watched *Cinderella* on video for the umpteenth time, my daughter, then 5, dumped out her few thousand crayons and markers onto the floor. While she worked in one room, I worked in another, oblivious to the fact that she was drawing not only on paper but all over the floor. It was a colorful mess. As far as I was concerned, I'd done enough housework for the day. So I gave her a rag and said that since she'd made the mess, she could clean it up.

Ten minutes later, the job done, she trudged in, carrying her bucket in one hand and the rag in another. Her indignation at having to clean up and her love of drama combined in the outfit she had quickly fashioned for herself—a bandanna wrapped around her head and paper patches taped to her dress. She stood before me and groaned, "I feel like Cinderella in this house. It's always 'clean this' and 'clean that.'" She was overstating her case more than just a bit.

Like most kids, especially most 5-year-olds, mine was only peripherally aware that housework existed, and that hasn't changed much in the intervening years. I've purposely limited most of her housecleaning-related education to reminders to pick up her own mess, and I rarely ask for her help with the general cleaning. Because we spend so much time in one another's company, however, she is regularly exposed to the steps I take to bring some order to our humble abode. Frequently, she pitches in with me playing Tom Sawyer. (Her: "Please can I vacuum?" Me: "When you're older. Oh, okay, but just this once.") Our system works for us.

Other families may have different viewpoints and different needs and prefer to assign chores. But no matter what chore policy a family has, home is where kids learn (or don't learn) how to take care of life's basic necessities. It's where they learn about money and budgets, repairing cars and remodeling kitchens, taking out the garbage, making beds, compromising, working toward the general good, sorting laundry and, cooking.

It's one of life's ironies that the more capable a child becomes at helping out around the house, the less willing she is to do so. Toddlers happily follow us around mimicking all the motions of housekeeping. But the marketers for make-believe tools and miniature vacuum cleaners wisely do not aim their sales pitches at older kids. School-age kids really do have better things to do than run a pretend wash through its cycles. Still, children need to be engaged in the processes of household management, if only because twenty years or so from now their spouses will resent you for never having taught them how to contribute to the maintenance of their home. What do they need to know?

Basic housekeeping. Use whatever method works for your family—a chore chart, a regularly set-aside time to tackle the week's housework, a daily 20-minute pick up—to key them in to keeping home and hearth together. At appropriate ages, teach them how to

It's one of life's ironies that the more capable a child becomes at helping out around the house, the less willing she is to do so.

77

work the various gadgets that were supposed to make housework easier, such as the vacuum cleaner and the dishwasher. Increasingly as they grow, give them responsibility for their own belongings. Teach them to respect your belongings, too.

Money management. While kids don't need to be privy to every aspect of your family's financial status, let them in on the basics of how your family manages its resources. Teach them about various kinds of banking and investment accounts. Let them know how money is earned, spent, saved, and borrowed. Let younger ones pay the cashier at a restaurant, including counting the change and figuring the tip. Let older ones write checks. If at all possible, avoid ATMs, which tend to give kids the idea that money can appear magically as long as one know the secret code.

Child care. Create opportunities for children—firstborns, last-borns, and only children—to learn about child care. While no older sibling should have major responsibility for caring for a younger child, no boy or girl should graduate from high school without knowing how to change a diaper, burp a baby, and safely entertain a toddler.

Household Hints

Here are ways around kids' natural reluctance to pitch in:

Work together. Most kids want our company more than they are willing to let on. Invite your child to help you do the laundry. In return, join him to collect the research for a school project. Just be careful not to insist that he disengage from a pleasant activity to help out, which equates housework with drudgery.

Offer a payoff. "If you help me get the dishes done, we'll have time to go out and get an ice cream afterward." This is not bribery. Bribery is paying a kid to do what's expected of him. A payoff of a fun activity with you or with others is a reasonable exchange, a fair return for the child's help. And while he's helping, he's learning a valuable skill.

Explain the tasks. Instead of simply having your children tag along while you shop, go to the laundromat or run other errands, talk about how and why you make your choices. Involve kids in making lists, setting and sticking to the budget, choosing purchases, and prioritizing chores.

Break down a job into its parts. Replace, "Clean your room," with a step-by-step approach: "Pick up the dirty clothes." When that's done, add, "Put your books back on the shelf," and so on.

Understand the motivation and offer reasonable rewards. It's a rare child who values neatness and who volunteers to wax the floors. When a child does help out, she's likely doing it to please you, and her contribution should be acknowledged with thanks.

A payoff of a fun activity is a reasonable exchange for the child's help.

When kids help out with a big chore, such as helping you run a yard sale, pay them over and above their allowance. Share *your* pleasure at completing a job, not just the unpleasantness of doing it.

Teach team playing. Help kids understand that each and every family member's input is needed to help the family function. Housework cannot be presented as punishment but as a necessary part of life in a matter-of-fact manner. Concentrate your efforts on getting kids to pitch in on communal spaces, where one person's mess really affects others. Let the rest slide.

ive all your children the opportunity to learn the skills they need.

Rotate jobs. Don't allow any child to get the label (and the limited experience) of "dishwasher" or "baby-sitter." Whatever needs to be done can be learned by each and every family member. It helps, too, to not label areas of the home as yours, as in "Don't walk on my newly waxed floor." Once you've claimed the space, anyone within earshot learns immediately not to worry about this area.

Assign tasks on a nonsexist basis. Few males can get through life without knowing how to do the laundry; few females can survive without knowing how to change a tire. Give all your children the opportunity to learn the skills they need.

Never turn away a volunteer. Sure you could do it faster yourself. But unless you always want to do it yourself, sign up whomever steps forward.

Don't criticize. If you remake the bed seconds after your child does, you undermine his contribution. A crookedly placed bed covering achieved by a child is preferable to a perfectly made bed by you. Allow kids their own methods. Learners need to do things their way and that may mean differently than you'd do it yourself. If you insist that your child mimic your way of doing everything, he will find it far easier to give up.

Adjust your standards. People who live in perfectly kept homes probably don't have children—or they have hired help. Most of us who have kids have learned to lower our standards somewhat. Kids need to know that we value the delightful messiness they bring into our lives more than we value a spotless floor. After all, who really wants to have a "floor so clean that you could eat off of it?" Yuck.

Respect private spaces. As much as possible, particularly for older children and teens, refrain from taking over the cleaning and organizing of private space. As long as there are no health-code violations and you have no legitimate concern about your child's well-being, learn to close the door—and your mind—to the chaos of a child's room.

> **READ MORE ABOUT IT**
>
> *Loving Each One Best,* by Nancy Samalin (Bantam)

18 Raising an Adult

Parenthood is not for sissies. One friend, the mother of an 18-year-old, put it well when another friend who was expecting her first child asked, "How long did your labor last?" She answered, "So far, for eighteen years."

There's no doubt about it: Raising a human being is a long-term project. There is, of course, the mundane business of feeding and clothing the kid and providing shelter for two decades or so. But that's the easy part. Guiding our kids in matters of the spirit—teaching them what it means to be alive, helping them develop the values that will guide them throughout their lives, inspiring them to reach for the brass ring—that's where the real labor of parenting comes in. And the real payoff. But the payoff can only come if we understand that the goal of raising a child is to raise an adult.

This is not to say that childhood is a mere preparation for adulthood. Every day of childhood is as valuable as every day of adulthood. What it means, though, is that if we limit ourselves to raising a child, we'll succeed, and we'll find ourselves someday with a 30-year-old son or daughter with the maturity of a 12-year-old. If, instead, we concentrate on raising an adult, we impart from the beginning the understanding that behavior matters.

The false dichotomy between childhood and adulthood begins with how we label various behaviors and how we categorize them as appropriate for children or for adults. The "good" child is obedient. None of us names "obedience" as the hallmark of a good adult, however. The mature adult, we know, acts from inner conviction. The same behavior we call "stubborn" in a child is labeled "tenacious" in an adult. And, depending on the degree of cynicism we're feeling at the moment, some of the very best human traits—exuberance, a sense of wonder, a deeply rooted belief in fairness, for example—are dismissed as "child-like," while behaviors such as thoughtlessness and rudeness are accepted as the natural shortcomings of children, things they will outgrow, somehow, before they reach legal age.

The truth is that the blindly obedient child grows up to be unsure of her ability to make a decision, whereas the child who's taught to be cooperative develops a lifelong habit of balancing her needs against the needs of others. The child who is permitted to behave in a self-centered manner grows up to be a self-absorbed adult. The rude child becomes a rude adult. The behaviors and attitudes by which we live our lives grow or diminish on a continuum. Rarely does anything happen at age 18 or 21 to change us—or our children—dramatically.

When we concentrate on raising children, we wrongly assume that our kids will adopt the attitudes and behaviors of mature people, without being consciously and consistently prodded toward that maturity. So it's important to know from the start what it is we value so that we can concentrate our energy on helping our children develop the qualities that will serve them and their communities throughout their lives.

It means paying less attention to the usual focus points of discipline, such as a

*I*f we limit ourselves to raising a child, we'll succeed.

messy room, and more attention to the inner workings of a child's character, such as a missed opportunity for kindness. It means letting our kids know that even more than we value their ability to bring home "A's" on their report cards, we respect and admire them for offering their seat on a bus to a person who needs it more than they do or their choice not to cheat on a test.

To help children become grown-ups that earn others' respect and whose company others gladly choose:

Teach values. Help kids learn to develop a moral perspective and to act on it. Model the behavior you want.

Encourage responsibility. Give kids as much responsibility as their development merits. Ask yourself if your child would benefit by doing something for herself instead of relying on you to do it. If the answer is yes, then let her do it, even if she'd rather not.

Keep your word. Nothing better prods a child to be trustworthy than to have had her own trust rewarded.

Make lots of connections to the extended family and to the community. A child who doesn't feel deeply rooted can't grow strong branches. Learning to cooperate, to rely on others, and to be relied upon can only happen when a child cares about others and knows he is cared about.

Insist on civility. Behaving with respect for others is the hallmark of maturity.

Don't be a wuss. We can't fear being unpopular with our children, nor can we be their friends when they are young. Their love of rap, knock-knock jokes, and action figures guarantees that they'll have to seek friendship from others their age who share these interests. We can't give in to all our children's wants and attempt to protect them from all disappointment and still guide them toward true maturity without frustrating their desires at times, without putting limits on their behavior, and imposing reasonable consequences for misbehavior. While we don't need to physically punish our children, to expect blind obedience to all or even most of our requests, we do need to let them know that we say what we mean and we mean what we say. (And we must be in the habit of saying yes whenever we can because a child who hears no all the time never learns to think for herself.) We must also be willing to renegotiate the rules as our children grow.

Don't rush them. Urging kids to perform beyond the level of their development only slows them down in the long run. Give kids permission to "act their ages," in the direction of their real abilities and ambitions. Pushing a 6-year-old to master a two-wheeler or a 12-year-old to practice dating tells them that their own reluctance to surge forward is inappropriate. It's not.

Honor maturity, not just age. Let children's demonstrated maturity open new gates, rather than bestowing new privileges simply for having a birthday.

Be adaptable. Life will inevitably toss curve balls. Help children learn to "go with the flow," to get up when they're knocked down, to find a new path when the planned route is blocked, and to embrace life after a loss.

Offer hope. Help children believe in the future and their place in it.

Help children learn to "go with the flow" and to embrace life after a loss.

85

Part 2:

Helping Children Develop the Character and Characteristics of Active Learners

19 Curiosity

nlike textbooks, life does not come with an answer key. That's why absorbing all the knowledge in all the books ever written would not be enough to get us through today. And certainly not tomorrow. That's not to say that knowledge isn't important. On the contrary, the ability to know is something that makes each individual more than a biological mass of cells, turns a number of individuals into a community, and makes communities evolve into a culture.[30]

But knowledge has its limits. Alone, it won't guide us to ask questions or to find answers. For that, we need unbridled curiosity. To be curious, a learner must first care. To care, he has to know that his curiosity will bear fruit—that he'll have the time to pursue a question and that his findings will matter. Increasingly, both schools and the business community rank the ability to question as far more important than the mere recitation of answers. Questions arise from curiosity. To foster it:

Let kids handle anything they can safely handle. A child needs to touch and handle the things that fill her environment. Walking through mud can't be something kids wonder about but never get to experience. With time and tools, few children can resist taking something apart to see how it works or mixing various ingredients to see what might happen.

Ask "what if . . .?" Model wondering about the world around you: What's inside? How does it work? How does one material interact with another? By doing so, you grant kids permission to do the same.

Note connections. How is a guitar like a violin? How is it different? What things in our house are the same as those used a hundred years ago? How are they alike? How are they different?

Don't rush discoveries. Your knowing the answer to something may make you want to hurry your child through his own discoveries so he can reach the predicted conclusions. But a child will understand better and remember more when he's given the time to find things out on his own.

Provide the tools to satisfy wonder. A tape measure gets kids wondering about how long something is. A magnifying glass, microscope, or telescope offer a closer look.

Provide adequate stimulation. Expose kids to sights and sounds, people and places. Only by experiencing interesting and varied stimuli can a child's brain grow adequately. A dull environment produces dull people.

To be curious, a learner must first care.

Encourage questioning. Don't be too quick to say, "Look it up" or "I don't know," which blunts any urge to keep asking new questions. When kids ask their questions, simply give answers when you can. Sometimes it helps to clarify what information a child is seeking. A "What do *you* think?" instead of a ready answer can uncover a lot about the workings of your child's mind. Usually, there's no need to go overboard with explanations. The 4-year-old who asks, "Where do babies come from?" will likely be satisfied with a very simple answer, such as "Babies grow inside their mommies." A 10-year-old needs more.

20 Problem Solving

*J*ust knowing that there are always more solutions than there are problems makes the world a more welcoming place. Solving problems is the outgrowth of curiosity and the precedent for discovery. To help your child become a good problem solver:

Play guessing games. Estimating and predicting give kids practice in testing their ideas. Guessing games can focus on observation and recall, such as asking your child to guess how many lamps there are in the house and then counting to check his guess. Another guessing game focuses kids on number facts: Have your child grab a handful of jelly beans and estimate the number he's picked and then have him count them to check his guess. Then ask, "About how many people could you serve if each person were to get three jelly beans?" To play with the idea of chance, ask him to estimate how many of the jelly beans he chooses will be yellow. Let a child know that one brick, for instance, weighs about two pounds. Take guesses about how many bricks each family member weighs.

Ask probing questions. In our technological age, we often depend on machinery and electronics to answer our questions. But what if there were no clocks and watches? How might we determine the time of day? Ask kids to think about the many possible alternatives—from observing the sky, to being sensitive to their body clocks, to studying shadows, to reading the tides.

Think of new uses for everyday objects. Only in America could there be a special cooking implement for hot dogs and nothing else! Perhaps because of our ability to invent and market such single-use contraptions, we've lost something of our ability to improvise. Single-use toys, too, limit the imagination and thus don't encourage children to use their problem-solving skills. The kid who has a toy cash register has a toy cash register. The kid who has a shoebox has a toy cash register, a table and a bed for dolls, a fort, a toy box to store his crayons, *and* something to color. Help kids think of new uses for the things around them, such as a cooking pot. Could it be a watering can for plants? A drum? A guide to drawing circles? A hard hat? A fishing net?

Challenge assumptions. Visual and word games force the mind to look at the world a bit differently. Try these with kids over age 8 or so:

1. What words or phrases do each of these represent:

$$\text{ecnalg} \qquad \frac{\text{mind}}{\text{matter}} \qquad \text{cycle/cycle/cycle}$$

Single-use toys limit the imagination and don't encourage children to use their problem-solving skills.

2. Without lifting your pencil, connect these nine dots with four straight lines.

```
•  •  •
•  •  •
•  •  •
```

3. Think of twenty-five uses for a paper clip.

Provide manipulatives to test ideas. Knowing that the area of a rectangle is equal to the length times the width is a helpful fact to know—and one that can be easily forgotten. Giving children experience in using concrete evidence to test the idea is far more likely to help them see for themselves what the idea looks like. For example, instead of telling a child that a 2′ x 3′ carpet covers 6 square feet, let her work out the formula herself, using concrete things like blocks or by creating a visual aid, such as:

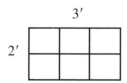

She'll discover for herself the relationship between the six squares and numbers 2 and 3.

Encourage making reasonable choices. We can ask a 2-year-old to decide if he wants to put on his mittens or his hat first, but we can't let him choose to forego a jacket in subzero weather. With older kids, the decisions we encourage them to make on their own require more wisdom on our part because the stakes are higher. We can ask a 10-year-old to choose which bicycle she wants to buy within a predetermined budget, but we can't let her decide whether or not she wants to wear a helmet when riding.

Step back. As we guide them toward opting for one action over another, we need to be available for consultation but not to take over. It's hard to let a child blow her allowance on a piece of junk that you know she won't want next week, but allowing her to do so—and not offering a few bucks a day later for something else she wants—allows her to go back mentally, rethink her choice, and use what she's learned the next time she has the opportunity to spend or save her money.

Resist the urge to be too rigid in making kids live with the results of their decisions. Part of learning is experimenting, and children should never fear trying out an idea. So, when she chooses not to wear a jacket and then gets cold, it would be cruel and counterproductive to insist she spend the rest of the afternoon chilled to the bone. Making a decision has to allow for reevaluation and a change of mind.

Limit opportunities for decision making. This is not as absurd as it may at first sound. The current wisdom is to give kids choices at every juncture, but this puts too much strain on everyone. Parents get in the ridiculous habit of negotiating with their kids over every activity. Kids, meanwhile, get the scary notion that too much depends on their input. Making a thousand decisions a day can overwhelm a kid.

Make sure children have the information they need. No good decision can be made without good information. This may require giving children information we may not be comfortable giving. For a child to make any decision about her life, whether it be what electives to take in junior high or whether or not to have sex, she needs to have facts, not simply rules and parental opinions, to make a good decision.

Encourage teamwork. Brainstorming with others gives everyone new ways to look at—and to solve—problems. Anything that must be done can be discussed, new ideas brought forth, and new ways of doing the same old thing can come to light.

Create new games and re-create old ones. Games that require strategy—checkers, chess, many card games, tic-tac-toe, and others—offer ample opportunity to plan and to revise plans, based on an opponent's move. Games like charades and dictionary offer every player a chance to lead the action. Making up new rules to old games puts a new spin on things. For example, once a player has learned the basic strategy for tic-tac-toe, the first player is either guaranteed a win or a draw, leaving the second player at a distinct disadvantage. Try this twist, suggested by Marilyn Burns, author of *The Book of Think*: Let each player place either an X or an O at each turn. The results are far more varied and the strategies far more involved.

READ MORE ABOUT IT

The Book of Think, by Marilyn Burns (Little, Brown and Company)

Raising a Thinking Child, by Myrna B. Shure, Ph.D. (Pocket Books)

21 Memory

Without memory, there is little self. It is the thing that makes our experiences worthwhile. We store impressions, data, broad concepts, and minute detail; and we reuse this storehouse of information when necessary. Sometimes, we need to recall specific facts for specific reasons. Students, particularly, need to be able to retrieve seemingly random facts for school success. Here are some ways to enhance memory:

Make the unfamiliar familiar. Before meeting with a rarely seen relative, show her picture to your child and talk about things you've done together so he has a sense of who this person is. Before traveling to a new place, read about it and review pictures together. Before reading a new book, teach kids to scan it first, looking over the pictures and chapter headings so that as the story unfolds, your child will have an easier time fitting in the new information with what he has anticipated.

Use memory tricks. It's not cheating to find creative ways to remember particular dates or names for a test or other occasion when memory seems to be removed from experience. Rhyming works for some people. ("In fourteen hundred and ninety-*two*,

Columbus sailed the ocean *blue*.") Acronyms can help some: "Roy G. Biv" is the name students are often taught to help them remember the colors of the spectrum—red, orange, yellow, green, blue, indigo, and violet. "HOMES" helps us remember the names of the Great Lakes—Huron, Ontario, Michigan, Erie, and Superior.

Visual imaging also can work: For instance, a child who has to remember to give a note to his piano teacher later in the day can be instructed to visualize his teacher eating a bowl of notes (either the musical or the paper variety). Then when the child sees the teacher this visual image comes to mind, triggering the memory that says, "Don't forget to give your teacher this note."

Play memory games. The classic card game of Concentration hones a player's memory. (To avoid too much frustration, start younger children off with ten pairs instead of twenty-six.) On long drives, play memory games in which the first player says a word, the second player repeats that word and adds another, and the third player repeats the first two words, adding one of her own. The game goes on as the list of words grows. Help kids learn the words to songs, which are also great memory-honers.

Practice memorizing. Memorization has gotten a bad rap, but it's a terrific shortcut to problem solving. The kid who knows instantly that 7×7 is 49 saves herself lots of time when she's working through a math problem. Kids and grown-ups both can enjoy reciting memorized poems or enacting a scene from a favorite movie. For added fun, tape-record or videotape the event.

Preserve memories. Help kids keep travel journals and make photo albums of special times and places.

Memorization is a terrific shortcut to problem solving.

22 Concentration

When it comes to paying attention, few of us *always* tune in and tune out when necessary. Most, however, are able to concentrate when necessary and to let necessary distractions (like an alarm) interrupt. Some, however, overrespond to stimuli and have difficulty focusing on any task for long. And sometimes, we adults expect kids to turn on and off according to *our* needs and abilities, not theirs.

For example, when a child is engrossed in an activity of which we approve, we're thrilled. We take pride when she devotes an uninterrupted hour to cleaning her room, working on a science project, or playing quietly. We're even happy when she's engrossed in a television program if it buys us an hour free from interruptions! We get annoyed only when we can't distract her to something else that we consider more compelling or more important. When she's too busy to come to the dinner table or do her homework, we get angry and impatient. When she's engrossed in something of which we disapprove, we call it an obsession. Clearly, "paying attention" is a virtue that's often in the eye of the beholder.

Sometimes, however, kids do need help paying attention—to teachers, to events around them, to you, simply because the social unit of the family or the classroom can't work well if each member is unaware of and unresponsive to others' needs. To focus concentration:

Encourage sensory observations. Using sensory data—how things look, smell, feel, sound, and taste—gives kids the means to understand and "make sense" of the world.

To strengthen visual awareness, ask your child to look around the room. Then have him close his eyes and recall specific things. What's on the table? What pictures hang above the sofa? How many bulbs are in the overhead light? The point is to get kids in the practice of noting details of their environment.

To sharpen aural awareness, play a "guess the sound" game. Take turns with your kids, as one player uses an object to make a sound while the others, who are blindfolded, try to name the source of the sound. For instance, the player who is "it" might crumple a paper bag, tap a pen on the table, or scratch the teeth of a hair comb, while the others attempt to identify the sound.

For "taste" tests, put a number of like-textured foods in bowls (bits of apple, slices of cucumber and carrot, for example). With each subject blindfolded and holding her nose, have her guess what you're serving. Then . . .

To demonstrate the power of smell, repeat the taste test, this time without holding the nose. How much improved is the guessing of which food is which?

To test the sense of touch, put some common objects in a bag and have each player reach in without looking and determine, by touch alone, what each object might be.

Using sensory data gives kids the means to understand and "make sense" of the world.

Give warnings that their focus will need to shift. "In 5 minutes, we'll leave the park, so get ready to finish your game."

Acknowledge your child's displeasure. "I know you'd rather be playing now, but you need to do this instead."

Teach list making. This not only helps a child focus on what must get done, it also is a first step in learning to prioritize.

Work on scheduling. Help older kids make a schedule to ensure that necessary tasks get completed in spite of distractions. Be sure to include their input. After all, if a child has a say in which order he does necessary tasks, he's more likely to comply.

Get feedback. Ask your child to repeat your directions and to write them down, if necessary, to help her keep her focus.

Prepare kids to pay attention. Ask pertinent questions and make directed comments before and after events. For example, before taking a trip to a zoo, direct a child's attention to what he might see there so that he can be on the lookout for it. Ask questions later to help him organize his memories of the event.

Allow enough time. When kids are engrossed in their own projects, knowing they won't be interrupted gives them the freedom to concentrate all they want.

If a child has a say in which order he does necessary tasks, he's more likely to comply.

23 Clarity of Thought

Thinking comes naturally. Thinking well requires some practice. Clear thinking depends on empirical evidence and discards the emotional clutter of things like prejudice and nostalgia. Mostly, it requires experience. To help kids use their experiences to formulate their ideas clearly:

Practice categorizing. Following day-to-day routines gives all of us lots of experience in categorizing. Invite kids to join you in any and all household routines. Let them clip and organize coupons, fold the wash and put it away, plan a menu, and help cook. Play card and board games, most of which offer multiple opportunities for classifying information. Visit zoos (where young children can observe reptiles and mammals and tell one group from another as well as differences and similarities within groups) and art museums (where they can learn to tell an impressionist from a surrealist).

On walks, enlist younger children to point out all the squares they can find in architecture and objects. Have kids organize objects into various categories. For instance, line up a blue toy car, a multicolored top, and a blue plastic spoon, and encourage them to make separate categories with the objects (in this case: "toys" or "blue things"). For older kids, make the categories more involved, such as helping them group three documents into two distinct categories. From among the Bill of Rights, the Monroe Doctrine, and the Magna Carta, kids can group the first two as American documents or the first and last as documents that guarantee freedom for citizens. They can apply categorizing skills to organizing their belongings, putting all game boards in one place, all schoolbooks in another place, and all clothing in appropriate places.

Teach the limits of categorizing. With their limited experience, kids can draw conclusions that more experience would not support. For example, if a child who has limited experience with dogs meets one that jumps on her, she will likely conclude that all dogs jump on people and all should be avoided. You can remind her that all dogs need to be approached with a certain amount of care but that not all dogs present a danger to her. You can help her broaden her experience of dogs by introducing her to a particularly calm one and letting her observe it from a comfortable distance. The new experience will help her rethink her original conclusion. Play some word games that help get thinking gears in motion: "If all fish are animals are all animals fish?" or "If all computers are machines are all machines computers?" In the broader social realm, teach in words and by example that prejudices and stereotyping are outgrowths of limited experience.

Discuss patterns. Look at how the color blocks are arranged in a quilt. Help a child notice how address numbers and street designations often follow a number pattern. Play patterning games. Lay out a fork-spoon-fork-spoon pattern on the table and have your preschooler figure out which item comes next. Discuss the seasons, weather patterns, the orbit of planets, the life cycles of plants and animals. Have your older child determine which number comes next in a pattern such as 1, 2, 4, 8, 16, ___.

Value ideas. In homes where ideas themselves are shown to have worth—where they are discussed, argued, negotiated, tried out—kids learn to play with ideas freely. When certain topics are off-limits, when disagreements are punished, or when conversation is simply limited, ideas die or, at least, go into hiding. Discuss politics at the dinner table, comparing and contrasting candidates' and family members' viewpoints. Seek opinions and evidence that backs up those opinions.

Use precise language. Because words are the means by which we classify and clarify, use precise language, and encourage your child to find just the right word to fit a situation or to describe an object or a feeling.

Encourage negotiating skills. The cycle of whining and giving in does nothing to teach a child to learn to formulate a good argument. Neither does authoritarian rule of parents, in which kids are doomed to failure if they try to ask for a new privilege or a new toy. But thinking (and family life) can be enhanced when parents help kids learn to present their cases well. A 14-year-old who wants to travel on the bus with friends to shop can learn that "everyone else is allowed to and you're treating me like a baby" doesn't do it. If instead he proposes possible alternatives (having an adult take them to the mall while waiting out of sight, having a practice run with you to assure you that he's ready

In homes where ideas are discussed, argued, negotiated, tried out— kids learn to play with ideas freely.

for the freedom and responsibility, or some other possibility) then he learns that thinking through your reasonable objections and responding with reasonable compromises helps gain the results he wants and that you can accept.

Uncover examples of muddy thinking. Sadly, they're pretty easy to spot. Advertisements, political speeches, arguments of any kind often contain examples of muddy thinking. My personal favorite is an ad I saw recently for blankets, which the merchant hailed as "genuine synthetic." In the selling of any product or any idea, there lurks the possibility that clear thinking has been abandoned in favor of expediency or attempts at outright deception.

Point out how advertisements, particularly those aimed at children, can misrepresent a product's worth. My favorite in this category is an ad for sweetened breakfast cereal, shown with toast, milk, and juice, in which the announcer says that the cereal "is part of a complete breakfast." It sure is. The only part of the meal depicted that offers little additional nutrition is the cereal.

Help kids see cause-and-effect relationships. If/then relationships are evidence that the natural world—and the social order—work according to set principles. *If* I don't feed the guinea pig, *then* he will die. *If* I don't complete this assignment now, *then* I'll have to do it later or *then* I will have to suffer the consequences of not having done it.

24 Learning Facts

There are two schools of thought regarding learning, which could be described as the Play-Doh vs. Plato positions. The Plato position emphasizes previously acquired knowledge, a.k.a. *the facts*. It honors the past as the model for understanding the present and for molding the future. It held preeminence from the start of Western education through the early 1950s. The Play-Doh position emphasizes the learner's experience, observations, and experimentations as the most important aspects of schooling. It hails the child as natural learner, as the creator and/or discoverer of knowledge. This position gained popularity in the postwar years and continues in a great number of schools today.

Recently, however, the facts are getting lots of attention—most of it negative—as study after study shows that American kids lack basic knowledge. A majority of high schoolers, one survey found, could not find Tokyo on a map. Some thought it was a state in the United States. Another survey uncovered that 30 percent of high schoolers did not know what event the Fourth of July celebrates.

Knowledge of history assures a common memory, a precondition for intelligent citizenship.

As a result of seeing the gaps (chasms!) of knowledge that some schoolkids suffer, there is a growing consensus that *what* kids learn is indeed as important as *how* they learn. Few, however, can agree on *what* that *what* should be. For instance, when asked "Is American history a subject worth studying?" most American parents would agree that, yes, it is. But then, should Columbus's arrival in the New World be hailed as the fruit of exploration and the opening of a new era of freedom and hope for oppressed people everywhere, the inevitable intermingling of cultures, or an act of aggression by European interlopers? The answer is not seen to be as simple as it once was.

Ironically, some of America's best ideals are the cause of some of our biggest dilemmas in teaching a subject as seemingly straightforward as American history. By embracing diversity, do we overlook commonality? By embracing tolerance, do we teach that all social structures and all political systems have equal merit and, thus, give short shrift to the culture in which students are growing up?

If knowledge is power, lack of it ensures powerlessness. Knowledge of history assures a common memory, a precondition for intelligent citizenship. The drama of the human experience offers proof that causes and effects are linked, that the past influences the present, and that embracing one value has a different outcome than embracing other values. The pursuit of cheap answers, wishful thinking, and avoidance of history's lessons always bring down the society that allows them. Those who create a false history—Holocaust deniers, for instance—find people to listen to them. Their spouting fills a void of knowledge. Knowledge of facts, clearly, makes learning meaningful. It can't be separated from the "learning how to think" approach. It *must* embrace the thinking.

The healthy skepticism that comes from questioning, from problem solving, allows learners to weigh issues, to hold or discard ideas that have historically been based on facts. Memorizing the preamble to the Constitution is meaningless unless students also know to ask, "Why do societies grow? Why do they fail? What conditions must humans enjoy and what work must be done to assure those conditions?" Facts are necessarily subject to critical thinking. The "fact" of the flatness of the Earth was debunked by those who were willing to question the assumption and willing to test their idea.

Learning deeply, not just broadly, takes hard work. It also takes exposure to the culture's best developments. An educated person must be flexible enough to let in the new; confident enough to preserve the old; and expansive enough to hold it all. This is no small order, but it can be done. Modern children's education may not cover all the material their parents or grandparents think it should. But it must demand that they learn more than how to think or how to feel good. What to look for in your child's schooling should include:

A clearly defined curriculum. Administrators need to make their goals for your child available and clearly understood by teachers, parents, and students.

A respect for content. Look over the books your child brings home. Be sure that the materials offer a range of culturally important works—literature, history, geography, science, and social studies texts that demand deep understanding. Passing the knowledge of one generation on to another ensures the survival of the culture.

An educated person must be flexible enough to let in the new; confident enough to preserve the old; and expansive enough to hold it all.

READ MORE ABOUT IT

The Unschooled Mind, by Howard Gardner (Basic Books)

What Your __-Grader Should Know, by E.D. Hirsch Jr. (Delta)—a series for parents and children from first through sixth grade, one volume per grade.

Cultural Literacy: What Every American Needs to Know, by E.D. Hirsch Jr. et al. (Delta)

Truth. Be wary of politically correct or otherwise skewed presentations. No matter what the book says, a study of Ecuadorian Indian village life is not the equivalent of studying the Magna Carta, if the lesson's goal is to understand the growth of democracy and its impact on modern life. So-called "balanced views" can be downright at odds with factual knowledge.

All texts are written in their own time and will naturally show precedence of one cultural position over another. Presenting a more modern version of events is not necessarily a bad thing. Tossing out references to Native Americans as "savages," a common practice in early twentieth-century texts, is just one example of how an updated position is an improvement. If your child's texts are overly laden with opinion, give him the opportunity to explore other, more intellectually honest materials.

25 Creativity

We tend to think of creativity as the making of something new or seeing the usual from an unusual perspective, but, in themselves, these are very limited definitions of creativity because they focus on the end while ignoring the means to that end. Simply looking different or behaving in eccentric ways are not the marks of creative genius either. Creativity is much more than what separates one person from another or one person's perspective from another's way of looking at things. After all, innovation and invention serve to bring us together rather than separate us. Creativity is even more than a mental state of heightened awareness. It is the passionate need to *do* something.

Watching a 3-year-old draw, a 5-year-old play at being a superhero, a 10-year-old immersed in the job of fixing up her bike, or a teen thoroughly focused on making posters for a political rally—these things allow us to see creativity in action. Put simply: *Creativity is the drive to make something, whether it be an idea or a piece of machinery, work.* It is the melding of curiosity and problem solving and it thrives in an atmosphere of trust and openness and patience. It has time on its side. It's always self-motivated,

Creativity is the passionate need to do something.

109

though others' encouragement can allow it to flower. It can be either highly private or extremely social. Creativity values the process as much as the result. Creativity is always fun, always, in fact, joyful.

By and large, children are creative. Their busyness is evidence that they are in the business of questioning and problem solving and doing. The ability to believe in the unseen, to access and live out their fantasies, and to wonder without embarrassment is the gift that nature bestows on children. It is up to us not to rob them of this gift, not to store their dreams like outgrown toys in the attic.

In the best classrooms, teachers have a passion of their own and this passion allows creative approaches to learning and doing. In those classrooms, however, where much class time is taken up with the need for teachers to input a particular set of data and for students to absorb a certain set of facts, creativity may get squelched. Learners need to acquire skills, but reducing all of learning to skill acquisition robs learners and teachers alike of the exhilaration that comes from discovery and expression. Even if your child's classroom is not a breeding ground for creativity, his own creativity can flourish with your support:

Give him the time and tools needed to pursue an interest. Only with these can an idea become a passion. Imagine if Steven Speilberg's mom had refused to allow him to work his moviemaking magic in their kitchen!

Respect your child's m.o. You may like to pursue the answer to a problem by discussing it with others. Your child's *modus operandi,* his way of doing things, may be

In the best classrooms, teachers have a passion of their own and this passion allows creative approaches to learning and doing.

110

to look at possible solutions and to work backward to test if this solution makes sense. A good motto is "whatever works, works."

Encourage playfulness. While certain things do need to be accomplished in the course of a day—homework, eating, housework—allow plenty of time for random acts of thinking, doing, and playing.

Don't insist on "well-roundedness." Sure it's important for children to be exposed to a wide range of activities and to have many and varied experiences. But a profound and passionate interest in one area will necessarily diminish time to pursue this variety. Respect and encourage the focused attention that grabs at your child's heart and mind.

26 A Moral Perspective

That prolific writer Anonymous offers these words of wisdom: "Children are a great deal more apt to follow your lead than the way you point." That's true—but only so far. The truth is that kids need some verbal pointing as well as a good example.

It's not enough to live a good life; to be fair, honest, and patient ourselves and to assume that our children will absorb the lessons. We've got to teach them, in words as well as deeds, why we live as we do and why positive qualities, even when they may bring short-term discomfort, are worth acquiring and worth holding on to. Without explicit teaching of right and wrong, without open discussions about what is good and what is not, and without clearly stated expectations and mutually understood consequences of falling short of those expectations, we may find that, like parents interviewed on a 1996 edition of the TV-newsmagazine *Primetime*, our children don't believe what we think they do and therefore can't act in ways we think they should.

In the segment, parents watched videotapes of their children responding to questions that probed their values. The children, all articulate, accomplished students who ranged from ages 10 to 14, were asked, for instance, if they would harm someone else for money. Shockingly, a number of kids reported that if the price were high enough, they would. The children professed a profound cynicism, a belief that their own needs and wants overrode all others' needs and wants, and an attitude that precluded even a basic notion that right is better than wrong.

"Do What I Say *and* What I Do"

By many objective standards, these were good children, high achieving and clearly comfortably living by the rules of middle-class American adolescent life. But they just as clearly lacked a moral center. It was frightening to imagine these kids a few years from now as parents, as neighbors, as part of the workforce. The parents, understandably, were extremely saddened by their children's responses. Each, however, admitted that he or she had not consistently shared, in words, his or her own values. Instead, the parents had counted on their own good behavior to model what they hoped their children would believe and therefore how they would act.

Living in an atmosphere of kindness and respect, of course, does go a long way toward raising kind, honest, respectful people. But children need to know, too, that their behavior is as important as ours. They need opportunities to practice doing good and making hard choices. And they need to know that our kindness may sometimes require that we let them suffer the consequences of their actions (or inactions) rather than expecting us to express sympathy for a natural result of the choices they've made.

Children need opportunities to practice doing good and making hard choices.

113

Equally important to monitoring our kids' behavior for signs of wrongdoing is getting into the habit of noticing when they've behaved admirably. To help bring out the values that contribute to their and society's well-being:

Share reasons for choosing positive behavior. We need to let our kids know why we make the choices we do. Upon finding that a store clerk gives us too much change, we can let our kids see us return it. Then they understand that we did so "because we don't keep what isn't ours." When we're working too hard at something that we must do, we can say, "I wish this project would go away, but it's my responsibility to get it done. And if I don't do it, I'll let other people down." Or "If I don't do it now, I'll just have to do it later, so I might as well stick to it." Let them experience with you the pleasure of fulfilling a responsibility, not just the hard parts of doing what's right. Kids need to know that being responsible is self-gratifying, not foolish or sacrificial.

Look for "teachable moments." When we're with our kids and see an act that inspires an internal response, put that response into words. Television viewing offers many, many such moments. For example, when a character behaves violently toward another character, ask, "What other ways could he have solved his problem?"

Ask probing questions. Find out what your child thinks about the big issues by asking questions such as: "What do you think is more important in life—to be honest or to be rich? Are honesty and wealth mutually exclusive?" Help kids sort out the opposing pulls on their minds and hearts.

Connect values to something larger. We didn't arrive at our values in isolation from other people or through concepts that originated with us. Children need to know they belong to a community of others who value the same things they do—a religious community, a country, a culture. Kids will have a much easier time understanding why they believe in an ideal such as freedom if they are helped to feel a positive association with their country and its history, including how their ancestors struggled to assure freedom for an ever-increasing number of people, and their own role in guarding that freedom for themselves and others.

A belief in the general goodness of their community gives children the freedom to embrace it as well as dissent from it in a positive way. Be wary, however, of teaching kids a meaningless pride in their heritage. After all, they are no more responsible for the good that those who went before them accomplished than they are for any of their failings. They need to understand simply that they owe something to those whose struggles and accomplishments preceded them. They can be honestly proud only of what they themselves contribute.

Never shame a child for misbehaving. Kids want to please us. Sometimes they can't be as courageous or as courteous or otherwise virtuous as they or we would like. Saying, "Aren't you ashamed of yourself?" turns a child's vision inward where their resentment and shame can seethe. Instead ask, "What better choice could you have made?" Making the personal choices that mature individuals must make grows with the child.

READ MORE ABOUT IT

Books for Children:

Aesop's Fables

The Children's Book of Virtues, edited by William Bennett (Simon & Schuster)

Books for Parents:

Teaching Your Children Values, by Linda and Richard Eyre (Simon & Schuster)

20 Teachable Virtues, by Barbara C. Unell and Jerry L. Wyckoff, Ph.D.

Understand development. Children need time to adopt values. Most will experiment with behavior that would be immoral for a more mature person, but is not for a child. Don't overreact to kids' confusion.

Act in ways we want our children to act. While actions alone can't be the only way we convey what matters to us, no amount of talking about our values will have an impact if our talk is not matched by our own behavior.

27 Kindness and Generosity

Beyond just being kind and generous yourself:

Find real-life examples. When we see someone on the street stopping to help a stranger by picking up a dropped package, say, "Isn't that nice how that girl picked up that lady's package?" Commenting on concrete, observable actions is more memorable than simply saying, "It's important to help others."

Act on beliefs. Whenever possible, *be* the person who stops to help someone out and encourage your child to help with the helping. If your local playground is a mess, organize a cleanup instead of wishing aloud that "*they*'d do something about the park."

Stick close to home. Let children know that they can accomplish a lot within their own close-to-home sphere of influence. A child who's encouraged to shovel out the driveway for an older neighbor after a snowstorm is changing the world in a positive way at least as much (and maybe more) than the child who's engaged in a letter-writing campaign to

Let children know that they can accomplish a lot within their own close-to-home sphere of influence.

117

Selecting a charity together can positively affect your child as well as the child your family helps.

save the dolphins. Taking on popular causes is nice, but it's no substitute for direct action. And experiencing immediate, positive feedback—seeing the driveway free of snow and accepting the thanks and respect of a neighbor—is a powerful incentive to making such acts part of the habit of living.

Involve your child in the art of giving. Regularly going through old toys and outgrown clothing to give to those in need helps a child view himself as a giver. As a family, putting money aside for important charities helps a child see that even a contribution of a few coins can grow into a worthwhile donation. Selecting a charity together, such as "adopting" a child through an organization like Save the Children can positively affect your child as well as the child your family helps.

28 Honesty and Trustworthiness

Children know that their ability to trust you is the most important aspect of your relationship with them. To help them grow in their own trustworthiness:

Help young kids differentiate between the real and the imagined. Most children lie at some point. Help the young tale-teller understand that "I know you wish an elephant had covered the walls with crayon marks. But since the elephant isn't here to clean up, you'll have to help me." As they're able to differentiate between reality and wishful thinking, the child who isn't taught to fear telling the truth and who has been taught to value the truth *will* tell the truth.

Praise honesty, but don't let it substitute for other responsible behavior. When a child does offer honest explanations, praise her honesty, but also present some consequences for the misbehavior involved. "Thank you for telling me that you colored on the walls. Because using crayons on the walls is against the rules, we'll have to put the crayons out of reach for a while. Now help me clean up the marks."

Teach the payoff for honesty. Older children are, of course, more adept at telling the truth from fantasy and will lie to get themselves out of trouble or to avoid work. A nickel for every untrue "I have no homework" or "I didn't do it" would pay off the national debt. Help children see that when they tell the truth, they earn your trust. They also earn their own self-respect. And truth tellers don't need nearly as good memories as liars do.

Reward trustworthiness. Get in the habit of giving new responsibilities and new privileges on the basis of behavior. Instead of "When you're 15, you can go to the movies by yourself," try, "Because I see that you can come home when I expect you to, you may go to the movies by yourself."

Keep your cool. When a child declares something that simply isn't true, or, more likely, denies responsibility for a wrongdoing or a mistake, try not to overreact. "I won't listen to you lie to me. We'll discuss it when you're willing to tell the truth."

Use logic. Help your child see the cost of dishonesty: "If you steal something, even something small from a big store, everyone has to pay higher prices to cover the loss and to cover the costs of security." "If you lie to me now, I will not find it easy to believe you the next time you tell me something, even if it's true."

Communicate that honest loss is worth more than dishonest gain. "At least I know he doesn't cheat," said one parent upon viewing her son's report card, which showed a list of Ds. (She added: "Either that, or he's copying his answers from the dumbest kid in his class.") Addressing the problem, she emphasized that the grades

*T*ruth tellers don't need nearly as good memories as liars do.

themselves didn't matter: "I want you to work hard and to be honest with yourself about how much you need to study."

Soon after, when the boy, who was 12, was given a copy of a book report to turn in, she offered him an alternative to cheating. "I know that writing the book report yourself will take hours and that it would be easier to turn in this report instead. I would rather that you get an honest B or C instead of a dishonest A." She made a deal: "You read the book yourself and write your own report and I promise not to be angry with your grade, even if you fail." He agreed and earned a C on his own.

29 Courage

It's important to talk about the people we admire and why we admire them.

There's a big difference between heroism and celebrity, but in an age when media is the message, kids need us to help them differentiate between fame and character. Help children see that heroism tends to be a quiet fortitude, not necessarily a single act of bravery, and is certainly not the equivalent of popularity. To help kids understand courage:

Introduce heroes. It's important to talk about the people we admire and why we admire them. Buying books and learning about people who have positively affected our world is far preferable to letting our children take the freedoms they enjoy or the inventions that enhance the quality of their lives for granted. They need to know about others who went before them, who worked to make the world a better place.

Point out close-to-home examples of courage. The child who resists going along with others who are teasing another child is courageous. She's risking the wrath of her friends in order to do right.

Share your own dilemmas. Let children in on grown-up struggles to choose to stand up for what's right, even at personal cost.

30 Tolerance

Sometimes, just being clear ourselves about what social mores we believe in can be difficult. For instance, as a society, we praise independence. Rugged individualism is said to be a hallmark of the American character. Popular though it may be, this perspective is, in fact, at odds with the reality of both the American experience and the American ideal. At our best, we prize tolerance, inclusion, compassion, cooperation, and interdependence. Even these virtues involve some dilemmas: Do we teach tolerance of behaviors we find unacceptable? Where do we draw the line? As one father said, "Do I teach my son to be so open minded that his brains fall out?"

In fact, we structure our lives and model for our kids a sort of hierarchy of values: tolerance is high on our list, but making moral choices is higher. Having manners is essential, but we can be more relaxed at home than in public. Cooperation makes civilization possible, but going along with the crowd can erode civility if the crowd itself is behaving uncivilly. It's through our interactions with society that all of our values are put to the test. It's only through other people that certain values even exist. The golden

It's through our interactions with society that all of our values are put to the test.

rule, doing unto others as you would have them do unto you, insists that we each be actively and positively engaged with others. Home is where the learning begins. But it needs to be practiced in public. Just as responsibilities include caring for those we know, it also involves caring for those we may not know, but whom we, nevertheless, value.

Tolerance is the virtue that may be the most difficult thing to teach our children, largely because we need to teach them also not to tolerate everything around them indiscriminately. Some guidelines:

They need to learn to be intolerant of intolerance.

Focus on individual behavior, not stereotypes. The key in teaching tolerance is to help children see that dismissing a person for his views, his appearance, or his background is wrong. Meanwhile, kids need to learn to reject certain behaviors, language, and hurtful attitudes. In other words, they need to learn to be intolerant of intolerance. That, of course, leads us back to their behavior—and our own.

Don't tolerate intolerance. How much meanness, vulgarity, and prejudice are we willing to overlook in the name of tolerance for our children? Do we laugh along with the racist joke? Say nothing when our child makes fun of another kid for being overweight? Hope the "phase" will pass when our teen zestfully quotes Hitler? Showing tolerance of such behaviors would only serve to foster a greater intolerance. As Edmund Burke said, "The only thing necessary for the triumph of evil is for good men to do nothing."

Pay attention to language at home. Sibling wars are perhaps the greatest reminders of intolerance at home. Maybe because they're so common and so expected, parents try to avoid the fray bred by intolerance. "You make me sick," tossed from one kid to another is an example of one child being wholly uncivil to another. From the earliest, parents have to help children learn to judge and comment upon a person's actions, not her essence. "You can tell her that you don't like it when she comes into your room, but you can't call your sister a fat slob." Of course, we need to use the same kind of discretion: Saying, "I don't like it and won't allow you to call your sister a name" beats "You're such a mean kid."

Uproot ignorance. Limited exposure to others with different backgrounds and differing views allows prejudicial attitudes to fill the void of knowledge and acceptance. What we don't know can be frightening and what frightens us can make us defensive—and offensive. Discovering the person behind the myth debunks the myth. Inviting a foreign student into your home can put a real face on an idea. When personal encounters don't occur, help your children find reliable sources of information for learning about other cultures, religions, and peoples.

Value differences. When a child blurts out, "Why is that man wearing such a silly hat," when she first encounters a person wearing a turban, use the opportunity to let her know that others dress according to the rules of their society just as she does. Help her see that there are at least as many things that link us as separate us. Also help her to see that her perspective is not the only one. Ask, "What do you think you might look like to someone from another place? How would you want them to react to your differences?"

Discovering the person behind the myth debunks the myth.

31 Empathy and Compassion

When parents make every effort to understand a child's feelings and to let her know that her feelings count, the child has the best chance of learning to acknowledge others' feelings and to act accordingly.

Respect feelings. If we teach a toddler not to bite by biting him so "he knows what it feels like" or hit a child for hitting her brother, or humiliate a child for any behavior or for her fears, we teach little in the way of caring for *another's* feelings. When a child's feelings are not respected, the only feelings she'll be aware of are her own.

Praise acts of compassion. When we comment upon a child's empathy and compassion for others—"That was so kind of you to offer your toy to your friend"—we put more good feeling into her emotional bank account, from which she can make the necessary withdrawals.

Create opportunities for caring. Kids need opportunities to share the compassion they have. Sharing it, practicing it, helps it to grow. Kids can feel frightened when they see evidence of need—when they see a news report about a natural disaster, when they encounter a person sleeping in a box on the church steps. The more we can help them help—by pitching in to a neighborhood project to help the homeless, by collecting cans and sending the proceeds to the Red Cross—the more they learn that their good actions can help offset the bad in the world.

Don't inspire guilty feelings. Children needn't be made to feel guilty for their good fortune, but simply that good fortune offers them the opportunity to help.

> The more we can help them help, the more they learn that their good actions can help offset the bad in the world.

32 Responsibility and Self-Sufficiency

i remember Sister Mary Somethingorother's booming voice over the loudspeaker of my Catholic girls' school's public address system: "WHOEVER IS RESPONSIBLE FOR THIS INCIDENT HAD BETTER TURN HERSELF IN NOW!"

The incident in question was pulling a fire alarm to clear out the school (and thus skip a math test). No one was foolish enough to volunteer what we all knew about the identity of the responsible party. In this case, as in many cases of grown-ups howling at children, being "responsible" held no appeal.

Responsibility is often equated with blame. No one seeks to be responsible when doing so has negative consequences. The aim, then, in teaching our kids to be responsible, is to help them see the positive consequences of accepting responsibility. When responsible behavior earns a child increased pleasures in life, internal satisfaction, more privileges, and expanded independence, there's reason to strive for it. Here are some ways to help them join in the goal of being responsible:

Give kids the opportunity to entertain themselves. The child who can busy herself knows that filling her time usefully is her responsibility and not the domain of a parent/social director.

Allow children to experience appropriate struggles. Because we are so crazy about our kids, it is possible that we sometimes expect too little of them, rushing in to save them from possible defeat whenever a challenge appears too great for them to handle. Overprotection, though it appears to be a kindness, is one of the best means of undermining a child's emerging maturity. Instead of habitually doing for kids what they can learn to do for themselves, let them exercise their struggle muscle. Encourage them to try out new skills, such as swimming or biking, even when you're afraid they might hurt themselves.

Don't hover, which clearly states that we don't trust them to succeed. They may surprise us—and themselves—with newfound abilities and new ways to approach problems and achieve the success they're after. The key to finding out where your child stands on the ability spectrum is to observe other children the same age. If the majority are doing for themselves what you're still doing for your child, you may be guilty of overprotecting her and thereby holding her back. Holding on to a child's babyhood may be fun for a while, but remember: Eventually you want your child to move out, and if you make life too comfortable for her now, she may want to stay forever.

Let a child experience the consequences of his actions and inactions. The kid who forgets to finish his homework night after night earns himself (not you) a failing grade.

Eventually you want your child to move out, and if you make life too comfortable for her now, she may want to stay forever.

Be supportive. If circumstances not of her doing make it impossible for a child to finish her homework (or other required job) on time one day, you can offer to help. A child does need to know that she's got someone in her corner when things are overwhelming. One neighbor told me how, many years ago when her daughter was a teen, she took over her daughter's paper route for two months while her daughter's broken leg healed. Not every parent can rise to such heights of support, but my neighbor's story serves as a reminder that sometimes kids need a way around specific obstacles.

Offer training. Once we've conceded that a child is capable of performing a task, we needn't back off and expect too much immediately. Give kids some help learning how to accomplish what they must. Show them how you balance a budget, for example. Walk them through the process. Be available for questions. And most importantly, let her do it differently if she chooses.

Resist offering tangible rewards. When a child learns to do what is expected of her in order to earn a piece of candy, a new toy, or other treat, she doesn't learn to value the intrinsic pleasure of living up to her responsibilities. And when you withhold the rewards, she loses her interest in performing.

Monitor responsiveness. Play "What If . . .?" games to help your child learn responsible responses to possible situations. "What if a friend asked you to tell a fib?" "What if your schoolbus took a different route home and left you at the wrong stop?"

Also carefully observe your child in situations for which the rules of safety and civility may not have been spelled out, and help him negotiate the new situation.

Don't rush your child. The child who is pushed to grow up too fast for him is more likely to fail at independence. If your 3-year-old isn't ready for nursery school even though the neighbor's 3-year-old is ready, don't force him. Next year will come soon enough. At each age and stage of their development, children will sometimes think they need to be doing what the perceived coolest kids in their circle are doing—from in-line skating in the street, to getting their ears (or other body parts) pierced, to dating. Give your kid permission to slow down, to act appropriately for his stage of development, and not to seek popularity and acceptance by others at the high cost of self.

Restrict paid work. Perhaps the biggest hallmark of the responsible person in our society is the ability to hold down a job. Therefore, we urge our teenage children toward the world of paid work, where they can prove to us and to themselves that they are capable of making it on their own. Oftentimes, however, working for pay gets in the way of a child's more important work of attending to schoolwork and after-school activities that have a bigger payoff in the long run. While earning additional money is something almost every teen can and should do on occasion, too many hours spent flipping burgers will be likely to interfere with schoolwork. Kids who are working tend to put an awful lot of energy and time into their work, often saving for big-ticket items such as cars that further distract them from school. They also believe that because they're earning their

Give your kid permission not to seek popularity and acceptance by others at the high cost of self.

131

spending money that they are more mature than they really are and are more apt to insist on an autonomy for which they're not yet ready. Try to limit paid work to weekends and summers as much as possible.

Help kids use the language of a responsible person. "It tipped over," says the child who just knocked over a lamp. "My homework notebook is missing," says the kid who's misplaced her notebook for the third time this week. Using passive language seems to be the best way out when you'd rather not admit, "I knocked it over" or "I misplaced it." Passivity seems to absolve the speaker of any fault, to make her nothing more and nothing less than an innocent bystander to the events swirling around her. But, after the brief reprieve it seems to offer, passive language also leaves a person feeling powerless to affect her environment; it victimizes the speaker, leaving her unable to imagine that she has within herself the ability to take charge of her life.

When children use phrases that place the cause for events outside of their control, help bring them back to reality. Saying, "I did it," helps them see plainly that they can alter their behavior so that the same thing doesn't happen again.

Keep reminders brief. Simply saying, "It's time to do your homework," or even just one word, "Homework," works better than launching into a lecture about getting homework done. Lectures get tuned out.

Model civic responsibility. There's more to being a responsible person than simply taking care of one's own business. Individuals within a society must also be responsive to the needs of the larger community. Personal responsibility requires becoming involved, even when that involvement includes some inconvenience or discomfort. It includes following the rules of civil behavior and taking part in activities that better the community.

Explain how the interdependence of a society works. Give children little lessons on how the close-to-home world works. Who does what? Follow the course of a child's favorite treat to let him know the many people involved, each doing a job, who work together to get his apple juice to the table—the farmer, the picker, the trucker, the packer, the grocery clerk, you. Who makes the books he reads, the toys he plays with? Relate the jobs that make society work to his own public responsibilities—paying for purchases, abiding by traffic rules, etc.

Speaking of responsibility . . . The words we choose to teach lessons in responsibility can make the difference between whether or not the lessons are heard by our kids. When a child who's been practicing ballet in the living room knocks over a lamp and says, "I didn't mean to," don't shout, "I told you never to practice here!" Instead, try, "I know you didn't mean to break the lamp, but this is my reason for having the rule about not dancing in the living room." If a child forgets to bring home an important paper from school, don't say, "When will you ever learn to be more responsible!?" Try, "How do you plan to get the assignment?" See that she follows up on her plan.

> **READ MORE ABOUT IT**
>
> *Love, Limits, and Consequences*, by Teri Degler (Summerhill Press)

33 Self-Esteem

Your kid is great. Well, at least she's trying. And so what if her tryout for the gymnastics team placed her squarely at the bottom of the list. You want to soothe her hurt ego. You want to encourage her to try again—maybe next year. Mostly you want her to feel good about herself. So, like a dutiful, modern parent, you lavish on the praise. "You're every bit as good as those other kids," you half-lie. (It's only a half-lie because you half-believe it yourself.) Meanwhile, your child is inconsolable and your attempts to make everything (especially her) all right make her feel even worse. *Where did you go wrong?*

The Self-Esteem Trap

Self-esteem is one of those issues that has grabbed parents and educators by the horns. Everyone agrees that it's good to have it. Everyone agrees that it's imperative that parents and teachers instill it in children. Most people even agree on what it is—an innate sense of worth and of worthiness, a belief in one's abilities. Logically, having high self-esteem should endow children with a "can-do" attitude, foster resilience, and help kids cope with life's many frustrations. Why, then, does *telling* kids to feel good about themselves usually backfire?

Because kids are not stupid. They know that parents' praise is not always based on any hard evidence. Telling a child that he's a great mathematician when he can't multiply fractions as well as most of his classmates can does nothing to get to the issue at hand: the good feeling that comes from competence. It would be far better to help that child develop math skills. Kids know that in order to *feel* good about themselves they have to *be* good at something.

Think for a minute how you would feel if a report you prepared for your boss was greeted with high praise—even though you knew it contained a serious addition error, that your assistant had provided you with data you didn't quite understand, and that deep down inside, you yourself knew that the report provided nothing of any real value to the company. Your first reaction might be "Whew—got away with that one!" Then: "My boss is a real jerk." And finally: "How long can I get away with this? I feel like a fraud." Kids who are undeservedly praised just for showing up rather than because they've actually proven themselves to have mastered a particular skill go through the same stages—temporary relief, a diminished confidence in the praise-giver, and, finally, a diminished sense of their own ability. This is hardly the stuff of self-esteem.

So, what should we do? To begin with, we have to acknowledge that feeling good about oneself—which is the popular view of self-esteem—is not always a good thing.

Kids know that in order to *feel* good about themselves they have to *be* good at something.

Should the kid who bullies a playmate feel good about herself? Should the child who copies test answers from his classmate and receives an A for his efforts feel good about himself? Clearly, not. We also have to acknowledge that the real world—the world in which our children live—does not reward effort but instead insists on results. We must encourage effort, even insist upon it. But praise it? That's confusing to kids. And useless.

In truth, it's better to teach a child how to tie his shoelaces than to snuggle up close so you can tell him how great he is while you're tying the laces. Most important, we have to understand that the real roots of self-esteem have nothing whatsoever to do with our efforts to teach it.

That's right. Surprisingly, research on self-esteem shows that it cannot be taught. Moreover, it doesn't have much to do with the popular "feel-good" approach to child rearing. Even competency alone doesn't guarantee high self-esteem. In a landmark study conducted by Stanley Coopersmith, Ph.D., a psychology professor at the University of California at Davis, Coopersmith found that children with high self-esteem—no matter what their socioeconomic background or academic achievement status—shared one experience: They all had parents who set firm rules for behavior and who consistently enforced those rules. On the other hand, those children who scored low on Coopersmith's scale of self-esteem were children whose parents gave them freedom to make and break their own rules. Some of these children were high achievers, but they still felt lousy about themselves.

Self-esteem is essential for active, engaged learning to take place. Learning takes place best when the learner feels empowered to learn, a process that oftentimes means

Children with high self-esteem all had parents who set firm rules for behavior and consistently enforced them.

coping with frustration, starting over, reevaluating approaches and goals, and reveling in accomplishment. It doesn't start with feeling good. But it can lead to it.

Building Self-Esteem

Have confidence in your child's abilities. It's not enough to express confidence. We've got to stand back far enough to demonstrate our trust in their abilities, not so close to pick them up each time they fall. A "you-can-do-it" attitude is one of the best gifts we have to offer our children.

Don't mix up praise and criticism. Telling your struggling mathematician that "your adding is much better but your handwriting still needs lots of work" is a double whammy. Save working on the handwriting for another time.

Resist making comparisons. One child's performance has nothing to do with another's.

Be a coach, not a judge. A parent's job is to be helpful, not to overreact to errors. When a child fails a test, it's better to sit down with her and work out a strategy for improvement than grounding her for a month.

Provide the needed support. No child takes to every skill with equal competence. If a child is feeling bad because she can't do something as well as she feels she should, help her learn. You may have to get a tutor. You may have to spend evenings running up and down the driveway with your child as she learns to ride a two-wheeler. You may simply have to remind her that learning is most often an incremental thing, and that competence comes bit by bit, not in one fell swoop.

Show respect. It's extremely difficult to attain self-respect without being respected. The child who is listened to, safeguarded, and whose opinions and actions are taken seriously knows that she matters.

Be consistent in discipline. Knowing what the standards are and what he has to do to meet them and what happens if he doesn't lets a child know you care enough about him to invest the time and energy needed to raise him.

Label actions, not kids. Telling a child that "your practice on the piano is really paying off" is more effective than saying, "Wow! You're great!" Likewise, saying a simple "Thanks for your help" is better than saying, "You're such a good boy for helping me set the table." He'll wonder if failing to set the table next time might make him a "bad boy." His sense of worth needn't be so fragile. Calling a child "stupid" or "lazy" is cruel and few of us would do it. But globalizing a behavior—"Can't you do anything right" or "There you go again!"—likewise reduces a child to his mistakes.

Help your child accept herself. "I'm stupid!" "I'm ugly!" "I'm a jerk!" Kids accuse themselves of things no one who loves them would ever do. When a child is feeling bad enough about himself to beat himself up verbally, a seemingly kind statement such as "Oh, no you're not" can backfire as he seeks to keep up his end of the argument. A better

The child whose opinions and actions are taken seriously knows that she matters.

138

response is to help him walk through the problem that caused him to mislabel himself: "What makes you think you're stupid?"—"I just spilled paint all over my report."—"Does spilling something make a person stupid? I spilled coffee yesterday, and I'm not stupid. It seems to me that you made a mistake. A mistake can be fixed."

When a child is feeling bad because she really can't do something well, help her see that her worth lies in more than her real or perceived shortcomings. "I know you wish you made the team. This might be a good time to concentrate on your other talents." Suggest that she ask a good friend to help her list her positive qualities. More important, remind her that putting in more work to develop competence is the surest way to meet her goal.

READ MORE ABOUT IT

FOR TEENS:
Growing Up Feeling Good, by Ellen Rosenberg (Puffin Books)

FOR PARENTS:
The Little Girl Book, by David Laskin and Kathleen O'Neill (Ballantine)

The Little Boy Book, by Sheila Moore and R. Frost (Ballantine)

Reviving Ophelia: Saving the Selves of Adolescent Girls, by Mary Pipher (Ballantine)

Emotional Problems of Normal Children, by Stanley Turecki (Bantam)

34 Friendship

No matter how academically talented a child may be, his standing among his peers is central to how he views himself.

You may be sending your child to school to prepare him for the "real world," where he'll have to balance a checkbook, read traffic signs, and, perhaps, learn enough physics to win a Nobel Prize. Your child, on the other hand, is going to school to hang out with his friends.

No matter how academically talented a child may be, his standing among his peers is central to how he views himself, how well he sets and reaches for his goals, and how well he enjoys life.

A ten-year study of 20,000 American teens (conducted by Laurence Steinberg of Temple University, Bradford Brown of the University of Wisconsin, and Sanford Dornbusch of Stanford University) shows that along with parents' influence, children's friendships affect their school performance either positively or negatively more than any other factor—more than school buildings, curriculum, teachers, books, technology, and social status. The child whose friends support learning will take school seriously and get the most out of her educational experience. The child whose friends disdain academics will disdain learning, too.

We parents often mistakenly view the social world of children as transitory and of limited importance. But learning to coexist in the world of people who hold different views and who may behave differently, to make moral choices, and to emerge from the crowd as a responsible individual are lifelong skills that have their roots in childhood interactions. Learning to make friends and to pick one's friends wisely is crucial. The benefits extend far beyond classroom performance.

Here's an age-by-age breakdown of some of the things that you can observe and suggestions for responding to the intricacies of childhood relationships:

Toddlers and Preschoolers

Studies show that even young children can form true friendships, as witnessed by a 2-year-old's visible delight in seeing a familiar playmate show up at the sandbox. Many of their friendships are orchestrated by their parents as kids play with the children you like and who are children of the parents *you* want to spend time with. Nevertheless even at this early stage, children show clear preferences for certain individual kids; they're drawn to those whose play style is similar to their own and avoid those whose style puts them off, such as biters or whiners.

What children this age learn from friendships. Peer interactions are how children hone their emerging social skills. Sharing and taking turns are concepts that need to be introduced now. Parents can play "taking turn" games to prepare children for the

Preschool is the age to introduce the concept of empathy.

playground scene. This is also the age to introduce the concept of empathy, letting children know that their actions have an impact on others. Talking about feelings, showing empathy oneself for the frustration that led to a child's misbehavior, taking a firm stand against hurtful behavior, and praising positive behavior go a long way toward instilling the necessary understanding that underlies acceptable behavior.

Aggression. Verbal skills are still limited for preschoolers and, as a result, they often resort to physical means of expression—pushing, grabbing, even biting. When your child is the aggressor, firmly and calmly remove your child from the scene of her misbehavior and remind her to use her words and not her body to express herself. Keep the time-out brief and give her a chance to redeem herself. If your child is the injured party, show her sympathy, but don't overdo it. Instead, help her learn to address the aggressor directly, saying something like, "I don't like it when you grab." By rushing in and saving the day each time a young child meets a transgressor, we undermine her own confidence in handling social upsets on her own.

Shyness. Some children easily join another child or a group of children; others hold back. Both styles are normal and are fundamental to each child's inborn personality. The child who is painfully shy, however, may welcome some intervention on his parents' part. Before an unfamiliar play situation, practice ways for him to introduce himself to others. Stay close by, letting him know that you're available but reiterating that you trust him to play with others. Invite one child at a time to your home, where your child will feel more at ease. Teach him skills, such as building a sand castle or catching a ball, that allows him to draw others to him. There's no need to push a shy child to become the most popular kid in his nursery school; instead encourage one or two relationships.

Social inappropriateness. When most of us see a sad person, we respond with empathy. We react to a happy face with a smile of our own. Children generally and instinctually pick up on the cues that others give out with an appropriate response. Some kids, however, don't read others' body language and need help learning, for instance, that other children resent their standing too close. These children can be helped by explicit instruction in reading emotional cues.

If your child seems unable to respond appropriately to the social scene, try these exercises: Draw a variety of faces, each distinctly showing an emotion such as happiness or fear, and ask your child to identify the feeling shown. Practice making similar faces yourself and having your child do the same. Discuss how different facial expressions bring out different responses in people. Practice, too, standing too close and at a more acceptable distance, telling your child exactly what you're doing and why. Likewise, help your child to listen to the words that other kids are saying and to determine how different tones of voice indicate different feelings.

Grade-Schoolers

Children in the 6- to 12-year-old range are free to choose their own friendships as never before. Increasingly, the responses of other children are as meaningful to them as are their parents' responses. In other words, no matter how much you love and accept your child, her sense of self-worth is largely based on her ability to form and maintain friendships outside the family. This is not a bad thing; it is a true sign that the child is ready to deal with the world, not just on your terms, but on her own.

What children this age learn from friendships. This is the age of rules, of winning and losing, of give and take, of finely honing one's ability to choose friendships based on more than convenience, of judging oneself somewhat objectively, by the standards of others. This is the time when loyalties are first formed and tested. Shared interests predominate as the basis for friendships. Competence on the playing field is rewarded. Being a "bad sport," a "tattler," or behaving too aggressively or too passively can land a kid outside the schoolyard fence.

Sometimes, helping children develop social competence means standing back a little while letting kids suffer the consequences of their actions and inactions in their relationships. It means intervening when necessary, perhaps with the help of school authorities, to keep a bad social situation from becoming worse. Parents can encourage kids develop social and other skills. The child who can do cartwheels in the gym earns the admiration of her classmates; the kid who's a whiz at doing magic tricks has an ace up her sleeve at social gatherings.

Helping kids choose friends wisely. It's difficult to help children to look at their friendships objectively. Peer loyalty can be fierce, even when children understand on some level that a particular friendship may be unbalanced, with one child always the leader and the other always the follower. You can observe and make nonjudgmental comments: "I notice that Jason always decides what you're going to do on Saturdays. You can remind him that you'd like to go biking this week." If you notice that your child is spending much of her time with a child whose influence you would like to limit, avoid overtly putting that child down. Instead, provide opportunities for your child to invite another child to a fun outing, thus giving another relationship a chance to grow.

Schoolyard bullies. Bullying was once viewed as a relatively harmless phase that many children went through. Now, thankfully, bullying is seen more for what it really is—an inappropriate act of aggression that has no place in the schoolyard, on the school bus, or in the neighborhood. Bullying children grow up to be bullying adults. The level of violence among bullies has escalated, largely because children's access to weapons and exposure to violence has increased. Consistently bullied children can be harmed, both emotionally and physically, and they, too, do not necessarily outgrow their victimization.

If your child is the aggressor or serves as a backup to an aggressor, you must intervene, and the earlier, the better. Punishing the child physically is not appropriate and will increase his need to humiliate others. Instead, help him understand that bullying is a sign of weakness, not strength, and that true power is an inner strength, not a brutalizing, intimidating force. Make sure an aggressive boy is exposed to gently strong men, who can teach him to be confident in his own growing humanity. If his anger and aggression are out of hand, seek professional help.

Help him understand that bullying is a sign of weakness, and that true power is an inner strength.

If your child is regularly the victim of a bully, review anything he might be doing to provoke the aggressive child. This is not to say that "he's asking for it," but rather to look for patterns of behavior that mark him as a likely victim, such as unnecessary tattling or crying more than is socially acceptable for his age. If his behavior contributes to his victimization, clearly he's got to make some changes. Help him learn to respond to a bullying remark with humor, which may disengage the aggressor. Have him practice saying, "I'm not interested in fighting" and walking away. Let him know that he doesn't need to defend his honor or yours in a brawl.

A victimized child needs to know, too, that he's not alone and that there are people he can turn to for help and that his need for help does not further mark him as a victim. He needs to grow his own friendships so that he's not singled out just by virtue of being without friends around him. He needs reassurance that other adults at home and at school will come to his aid and, perhaps, confront the bully for him. If the bullying has been long term and affects his mood and sense of well-being, he needs the opportunity to get out of the situation, even so far as to transfer to another school.

Cliques. The social scene in schools often consists of two groups: an inner circle and everyone else. Many children form exclusive kinds of friendships that draw their strength from keeping others out. The clique's exclusivity is heightened by the outsiders' willingness to do almost anything to get inside. To keep this dynamic going, the clique will occasionally and briefly allow an outsider in to reinforce their power as the elite gatekeepers. In a typical clique-driven scene, the "in" girls will hang out together after school or during recess. Two other girls will pass their way and one will be invited to join the clique for that afternoon's activity.

The chosen girl is faced with a dilemma: Does she follow her heart's desire and go off with the socially prominent kids or does she stick with her friend and spurn the group? No matter what she decides, she's been zapped by the clique mystique. She either compromises her true friendship by abandoning her friend or she loses her chance to experience life with the "popular" set, even if only until the clique's next whim. True, some kids don't care at all for this scene and are able to avoid it with confidence. A great many, both inside and outside the circle, however, are hurt by the effects of cliques.

If your child is part of the "in" crowd, help her to understand that her actions can be hurtful, that the "group-think" required of those in the clique requires her to suppress other ideas and feelings she may have. Rather than being empowering, this is actually quite limiting. Make it clear that within your home you will not permit your child's fun to be at another child's expense. If she's abandoned long-term friendships for the approval of her new friends, help her to see that she's likely losing more than she's gaining; let her know that it's okay to have friendships with a wide circle of children, not just those to whom others have given their stamp of approval. At the same time, encourage her to expand her circle of friends to the point that the "in" crowd is also welcomed into your home.

If your child is suffering from the exclusion of other children at school, help her develop one or two close friendships with other children outside the group. If she's been

Make it clear that within your home you will not permit your child's fun to be at another child's expense.

147

excluded from a gathering to which "everyone else has been invited," such as a birthday bash, don't seek to diminish her hurt feelings. Avoid glossing over the exclusion with a "you don't need them" dismissal of the event. In fact, at this moment, she really does need to feel included. What can you do? Return to her some of the power she's lost by asking her for an objective assessment of why she thinks she may have been excluded. Thinking about the reasons for being spurned by the group—things such as not wearing the "right" clothes, being an A student if the group disapproves of scholarship, being unwilling to participate in some of the groups' activities of which she disapproves—may help her come to realize that the groups' approval comes at too high a price. Or she may find that there is something she is willing to change in her behavior—such as not talking sarcastically if that has annoyed any members of the group—if that will help her socially.

When your child is hurt, it's easy to dismiss those who did the hurting as unworthy of the child's attention. However, in the school world, as in the adult world, learning to get along with others is as critical a skill as is learning to resist the temptation to compromise one's values for group approval.

Teens

A teen's friends are the mirror that tells him it's okay to look and feel so differently from the way he once looked and felt. Peer identity is the necessary first step to declaring himself a separate person from his family, a safe hand-holding before leaping headlong into adulthood alone.

What teens learn from friendships. While the big values—choice of religion, choice of college—remain under the domain of parents, teens get their smaller values from their friends—knowledge about fashion, music, drugs, alcohol, and sex—things about which teens assume parents have no relevant knowledge. Teens get encouragement to try things that their parents wouldn't suggest—for anything from taking tuba lessons to inhaling glue.

Helping teens choose friends wisely. Because so much does depend upon teens making good choices in friendships, parents have to stay involved (as invisibly as possible) in their teens' relationships. Parents need to make peer pressure work for their kids. As David Elkind, author of *Parenting Your Teen* says, "Peers fill a power vacuum only if kids are not well parented."

Teens will not abandon the values you've taught them all these years simply because another teen urges them to do so, provided you remain active in their lives. You can do more than just hope they will be okay. You can make your home available to your children's friends. Parents can also make sure kids have access to a variety of groups of kids, not just school friends, by offering them time away at camp, membership in clubs, and the like. When a child knows that she has choices in her friendships, she's less likely to succumb to any negative pressure from the only available crowd.

Many kids find relief from peer pressure by blaming their parents. Give your kids permission to say, "I'd love to smoke that thing but if I did, my mother would kill me." It's easier to be uncool when a kid can blame her parents for her stance.

READ MORE ABOUT IT

Parenting Your Teen, by David Elkind (Ballantine)

Beyond the Classroom, by Laurence Steinberg (Simon & Schuster)

You and Your Adolescent, by Laurence Steinberg (HarperCollins)

Girltalk, by Carol Weston (HarperPerennial)

Teens have never looked good to their parents.

It also helps to resist passing judgment on teens and their friends simply based on appearances. Teens have never looked good to their parents. Likewise, parents need to keep reactions respectful and listen to teens' points of view when they learn that a child's friend has done something, such as drink and drive, of which you rightly disapprove. Parents needn't abdicate or, worse, try to be cool about it. Instead, you need to keep talking, all the while picking your battles very carefully. Most important, you can't get out of your teenager's life just because he tells you to.

35 Manners and Civility

Manners are more than trivial niceties. They are the actions that show that we care for one another. From the time children can talk, it's important to teach them basic rules of manners, primarily by modeling the behavior we want.

Avoid power plays. Saying "please" and "thank you," table manners, and phone and conversation rules, such as limiting interruptions, need to be introduced early. It's important, however, not to make perfect compliance an issue at home. Kids and parents can inadvertently get into a power struggle if each request from a child is met with a "What's the magic word?" kind of grilling. A method that works without any power struggle is to offer reminders, not demands: If, for instance, your child says, "I want a cookie," instead of saying, "I'll give you one when you say, 'please,' " try, "I like it better when you say, 'please.' " Then, whether or not your child complies, give him the cookie (if you would have anyway).

Accept a child's limitations. Help children with their compliance—keep a box of toys near the phone so that your toddler can play in your lap when you want to talk on the phone. Don't expect a 6-year-old to write long thank-you notes; accept a line or two and a signature. Don't drag a child along to adult-only functions where his childish behavior will inspire lots of correction. While you shouldn't bribe a child into good public behavior, you can offer nontangible rewards: "I know that shopping all afternoon is difficult for you, but if we can get through my errands without a fuss, we'll have time to go to the park later."

But don't excuse rudeness. Children may need reminders to say, "Hello," and to wait patiently when you stop to talk with a neighbor, rather than being allowed to pull on your sleeve, whining, "I want to go *now*." Encouraging politeness is the first step in helping kids know that though they may be the center of *your* world, they are not, in fact, the center of *the* world. Encourage the common gestures of courtesy from a young age: a 6-year-old can certainly hold the door for the person entering behind him; he can take his turn in line instead of wheedling into a closer-to-the-front spot. He can carry the packages of an older person. Help him make good public behaviors habits.

Prepare for the unknown. Before entering into a situation in which your child's need to be civil can be greater than his experience has prepared him, rehearse the upcoming event. If you're going to a birthday party, for instance, say, "Today it's so-and-so's party and the gifts are for him." Then practice having your child give away a gift. Children will need preparation for many occasions—restaurant meals, weddings, and shopping trips—any place where they'll be among others who have no reason to delight in their tearing through the room flinging French fries.

Catch them being well-mannered. Never miss an opportunity to compliment your child for good behavior. Hearing, "I really liked how you let me talk on the phone without interrupting," is the best reward a child can get for remembering to be courteous.

READ MORE ABOUT IT

Books for young children:

Pooh's Little Etiquette Book (Dutton)

The Bad Good Manners Book, by Babette Cole

What Do You Say, Dear? by Sesyle Joslin (HarperCollins)

Books for parents:

Miss Manners Rescues Civilization, by Judith Martin (Crown)

36 Appropriate Responses to Authority

"**M**om," the 12-year-old said as her mother drove at 75 miles per hour (in a 50-mile-per-hour zone) down the nearly deserted roadway. "What do you want me to do—watch out for the troopers or tell you to slow down?" A friend related this anecdote after she and her daughter returned from a weekend road trip. "I had to laugh," my friend, who prefers to remain nameless, said. "I really wanted her to watch out for the cops, but I knew the correct answer was b."

We all know the right answers when it comes to raising civilized, respectful children. It's hard sometimes, however, to live up to our ideals in ways that help our children adopt the values we purport to hold dear. Being respectful—of the law, of one another—is not always convenient or comfortable, but without respect, we have nothing. Predictably, respect begins at home:

Be comfortable with your authority. As in most things, the middle ground is usually the best when it comes to using parental authority. The too strict, overly authoritarian parent who seeks to break a child's will by demanding complete compliance, who is punitive and uneasy with a child's appropriate immaturity risks raising a child who either acquiesces too easily or who develops a defiant don't-get-caught attitude. The overly permissive parent, who neglects to set and enforce rules, risks raising an insecure brat.

The authoritative parent, on the other hand—the one who insists on high standards of behavior within reasonable boundaries—has the best chance of raising an individual who can live freely within a civilized society and who can live comfortably within his own skin. This child knows his needs will be attended to as surely as he knows that his are not the only needs that warrant recognition and attention. Cooperation is a choice. Obedience requires a guard to enforce it.

Let children know that adults, too, are subject to rules. Children learn early on, through observation and what we tell them, that people, such as a police officer directing traffic, commands cooperation. They learn, too, that everyone, not just them, is subject to rules.

It's important that we teach our children why we abide by society's rules and agree to the authority of others under a wide range of circumstances. We can ask them, "What would happen if drivers ignored red lights?" "What would happen if children didn't listen to the teacher?" We can also help them understand that authority can be questioned and disobeyed when necessary. "If you feel something is wrong, don't do it, and then tell me about it."

Share your responsibility for your children. Some parents worry that teaching their children to follow other adults' lead will undermine their safety. "I don't want Colleen thinking that just because an adult tells her to do something that she should do it," says one mom I know. She has a point, of course. We don't want our kids to be fearful of authority, so submissive that they'll become prey to adults who don't have their best interests at heart.

Under most circumstances, kids are smart enough to absorb the idea that they are expected to comply to the needs of society without putting themselves at risk or doing wrong. Nevertheless, a child needs to know that saying, "You're not my mother and you can't tell me what to do," to a friend's parent when he's jumping on that family's sofa, is disrespectful, not precociously independent.

Keep your feelings of disrespect for the authority figures in your child's life to yourself. If we let a child know that we think the teacher is dumb and the principal is a fool, we can't expect our children to take them too seriously. It's one thing to say, "I would have accepted that answer you gave on your test, but I'm not you're teacher." It's wholly another thing to say, "That teacher doesn't know a thing." Learning to cope with a seemingly unfair or less-than-perfect teacher is simply another lesson that school offers. If there's real incompetence, you'll have to do something, but don't devalue the job of teaching because your child is having a temporarily bad experience in a classroom.

37 Adaptability and Resilience

*C*hange is inevitable. Some changes—losing a good friend, a divorce in the family, moving—are particularly stressful, especially to children. Some kids who suffer an emotional trauma respond with depression, misbehavior, social isolation, and learning difficulties. Others in similar circumstances, however, bounce back.

So much of our pleasure depends on the attitudes we bring to each situation. Those who see success, satisfaction, and survival as achievable usually succeed in achieving these things, even in stressful situations. Those who feel that circumstances alone determine their state of mind feel powerless.

There are two key differences between the two responses. The first, and, perhaps most important, is that the resilient, adaptable kid has a strong bond with someone—a parent, teacher, coach, grandparent, friend—whose support helps him pull through. Along with support, the resilient child's ally offers strategies for looking forward, for shifting focus from the unpleasant now to a brighter future. Such strategies show that happiness is not an immutable condition, not a trait you either have or don't have.

The child's ally offers tools to achieve equilibrium: learning to look on the bright side, talking positively about the child and about the future and helping him to do the same, overriding negativity and negative comments with positive messages.

When a child claims "I'll never have another best friend. My life is ruined" after a friend moves away or "I failed the test; I must be stupid" after a poor showing at school, the ally offers a counter, positive argument: "It's hard to have a friend move away. But in time you will make another friend. If you work at that friendship, you may surprise yourself and enjoy time with him." or "A stupid person could never have figured out how to fix the VCR like you did. Failing one test does not mean you won't pass the next one." The ally offers examples from her own life or the life of some other person who matters to the child about achieving happiness after a disappointment or a serious trauma.

The child's ally offers tools to achieve equilibrium.

38 Optimism and Hopefulness

is the light at the end of the tunnel a sign that troubles are coming to an end—or is it the headlight of an oncoming train? In life, we always choose how to interpret the light.

While there's evidence that people are genetically programmed to a certain "happiness set point"—with some people naturally optimistic and others nascently pessimistic—the greater truth is that all people can learn the mental exercises that make pleasure and joy possible. To be hopeful, children need to believe in the future, not just theirs but the world's. Parents and teachers inadvertently teach children cynicism and despair, often with mistaken attempts to "empower" them to affect the future.

We rob children of hope in the future, in *their* future, when we teach them that the world's ozone won't last their lifetime, that all those cuddly-looking rain forest animals they love are doomed to extinction, and that the world's resources can't support the future population. This is not to say that kids can't learn of the world's problems. They should, of course. But that learning *must* be accompanied by an equal dose of information about what measures are being taken to fix the problem now to protect their future.

Children can learn to contribute to the problem solving, but not that they alone are responsible for cleaning up after previous generations' mistakes.

Each generation has its problems; each generation has done some ridiculous things to children in an attempt to address those problems. (In the fifties, I and thousands upon thousands of my age-mates hid under our school desks to practice what to do in case of nuclear war! We knew this was crazy—and useless. It was also terrifying.) Each generation has also solved countless problems. Kids need to learn in equal doses about the trials of past times and the solutions people created, the diseases that have been conquered, the ecological disasters that have been corrected, the wars that the good guys have won.

Almost as bad as teaching children that the future is bleak is waxing nostalgic about "the good old days." To our children, *these* are the good old days. While it's wonderful to share our good memories of our own past, we can't communicate that all good times are gone and the time of their childhood is tainted.

A poll conducted in the early nineties by *Scholastic* magazine of children in grades 3 to 12 revealed that 54 percent of the respondents expected their lives to be worse in ten years than they were at that moment. This is a tragedy. But just as children have been taught to be pessimistic about their future, they can be taught optimism. There's a huge payoff to an upbeat outlook.

Multiple studies show that positive thinking improves health, increases happiness, enhances self-esteem, and raises school performance. One study conducted by C. R. Snyder, Ph.D., of the University of Kansas in Lawrence, showed that the level of hope a

To our children, *these* are the good old days.

159

freshman had at the beginning of freshman year of college was the best predictor of the student's success in college, more accurate than the student's SAT score or high school grades. The most hopeful freshmen had the most successful college experiences, earned higher grades, and were more likely to graduate than their more pessimistic peers.

Optimistic kids have learned to see setbacks as temporary challenges, not as permanent conditions. For instance, the child who interprets an argument with a friend as proof that "nobody likes me" can learn to see the event in less global terms: "Maybe my friend is in a bad mood today and that's why we had a fight." Or, "Maybe when I told her that I didn't like her new haircut, I made her feel bad. I'll apologize." The optimistic responses recognize that bad feelings are transient. They define the moment, but not the self. Parents can teach children to reframe their thinking from globally depressive to optimistic and by doing so teach children to draw on their other qualities, such as empathy for another's feelings, responsibility for one's actions, and ability to work toward goals.

Parents can also help a child become her own best defender, to talk to herself as she would to another who put her down. You can say: "If I told you that 'nobody likes you,' you would tell me about all the friends you have, the parties you've been to, and the plans you and your friends have. So defend yourself *to yourself* in the same way you would defend yourself *to me*." You can ask probing questions to get to the heart of your child's argument with her friend so that she can see that the argument belongs to the moment but does not define her ability to have friends: "Do you think your friend is upset because

READ MORE ABOUT IT

The Optimistic Child, by Martin Seligman, Ph.D. (Houghton Mifflin)

you made the Chess Team and she didn't?" By learning to see the reality behind the argument instead of interpreting it as a life condition, your child can regain her optimism.

Another aspect of optimism is a belief in one's own ability to solve problems and to be good at something. When you let your child struggle to achieve a goal instead of jumping in to "help," you let her learn the "I can do it!" attitude she needs. *Your* optimism about your child's chances of success is contagious.

39 Emotional intelligence

Emotional intelligence flowers in self-control.

Nice guys (and girls) *do* finish first. A study by Bell Labs found that the most productive engineers at the company were not those who scored the highest on tests of knowledge or who had the highest IQs. Rather they were the workers whom others deemed as the "friendliest," those who could be relied upon to be cooperative, empathetic, and helpful; who could persuade, not bully; who could embrace others' ideas; who displayed positive emotions while keeping emotions such as anger and hostility at bay.

Emotional intelligence (EQ), a term coined by Peter Salovey, a Yale psychologist, and John Mayer, of the University of New Hampshire, and popularized by Daniel Goleman in his book by the same name, begins, say the researchers, with self-awareness. It flowers in self-control.

A scenario: We're driving along the highway when another driver cuts us off. Most of us would feel an initial anger toward that driver. The person who has a high degree of EQ would stop and think, "Okay, we're alive. No harm done," and would continue on her way. A person with less EQ would react, "How dare he! I'll get him. People like that don't belong on the road!" and would let her emotions spiral out of control. She would not be able to recognize her anger as something about which she could do something other than let it build. Her emotional reaction would not include the brakes of thought, the insight that reminds her to evaluate a situation and to seek the best solution. Where emotions reign, bad decisions are made.

Like IQ, some are born with a higher level of emotional intelligence than others. Infants with high EQ have been shown to respond with empathy to another's cries. These children are more likely to become popular on the playground, to see others' points of view and thus be fair-minded, not to take others' emotions personally, to delay gratification, to be optimistic. In other words, they're nicer.

A person with high EQ does not so much suppress emotion as handle it. He feels his anger, he recognizes it, he accepts it, and, most important, he gives himself a break from it. He uses coping skills—a good physical workout, counting to 10, thinking it through, for instance—to get past it.

EQ bears no direct relationship to IQ. Some people have lots of both; some have little of either. Some have high EQ and more moderate IQ; some intellectual geniuses can't socialize meaningfully. Unlike IQ, which can be measured on a precise scale such as the Stanford-Binet test, there's no numerical absolute for EQ. A number of tests, however, have been developed to determine the level of various positive traits. For each of these tests, higher degrees of the trait were proven to correlate to higher levels of life achievement (as judged by such things as professional level) and life fulfillment (as judged by such things as the respondents' own sense of happiness and the stability of their relationships).

Even children not born with high EQ can learn a repertoire of emotionally sensitive responses to others. They can learn to read their emotions as well as the emotions of others. Most important, they can learn to control their emotions, to apply the brakes when they sense themselves feeling an emotion that won't serve themselves or others.

Even children not born with high EQ can learn to apply the brakes.

A Positive Outlook

The more optimistic you are about your chances of success, the more likely you'll experience success. That's the premise borne out by a test devised by Martin Seligman of the University of Pennsylvania and author of *The Optimistic Child*. In testing Met Life sales-position applicants, Seligman had them respond to a series of questions that probed their levels of optimism. For example, respondents were asked to choose which of two factors explained a perceived failure:

You gain weight over the holidays and you can't lose it.
• Diets don't work in the long run.
• The diet I tried didn't work.

Those who attributed their failures to some innate weaknesses in themselves or in some global condition over which they had little control, he found, were not good candidates for the job. Those who attributed failures to specific things within their power to change, however, proved to be superachievers.

Friendliness (empathy, graciousness, social awareness)

A higher level of what might be called friendliness also brings rewards of success. In a test developed by Robert Rosenthal of Harvard, called the PONS (profile of nonverbal sensitivity), subjects are shown a film with nonverbal images of anger, love, excitement, fear, and other emotions. By reading body language alone, subjects determine the feeling behind the image. Those who could correctly identify the feelings proved to be more popular and successful than those who were insensitive to nonverbal cues.

Children learn to read emotions at a very young age. When the emotional face (a smile, for instance) matches the emotional content they experience (kindness), they become good judges of others' feelings. When there's a mismatch—when, for instance, a parent smiles while yelling at a child—his ability to recognize nonverbal cues is greatly reduced. When children experience major shifts in the emotional climate, when a parent reacts with hugs one second and then shifts to anger the next, the child's fix on emotions is upset.

Self-Control

Another test, the famous "Marshmallow Test," shows that children who lack self-control, who at age 4 are impulsive, grow up more likely to drop out of school, have poorer quality social relationships, and become violent (for boys) or pregnant (for girls). Kids who showed self-control grew up happier and more successful.

In the test, the child is seated before a marshmallow and asked to refrain from eating it. When the researcher leaves the room, some children immediately gobble up the treat. Some wait a few minutes, but soon give in to the temptation. Others struggle to control themselves and manage to wait. Those who waited were the children who, when tracked sixteen years later, had multiple successes in their lives—high academic achievement, positive social connections, and general happiness. Their more impulsive peers had the habits and reality of failure.

Helping children learn the benefits of self-control and patience relies primarily on the level of trust they have in adults. Those whose parents tell them the truth, who keep their promises, who reward their children's patience, and who expect and maintain high standards of behavior raise happy, productive kids. These children may not be the most intellectually gifted, but they are the most successful. To raise your child's EQ:

Be respectful of the child's feelings. Shaming a child for being afraid to dive into the deep end of the pool only adds shame to his feelings of fear. Criticizing harshly and personally makes it nearly impossible for a child to see that he has control over a situation and can overcome a failing. Saying, "You're such a coward," creates an incredibly high barrier for the child to climb. Saying, "Remember how you learned to ride a bike after practicing. I'm sure the same will happen with your diving. You'll know when you're ready. And when that time comes, I know you can do it."

Help children recognize and name their feelings. By helping a child recognize, name, and accept her emotional life, she develops the self-awareness necessary not to be overpowered by emotions. Saying, "I know you're sad. It is sad when a pet gets sick and dies," validates what she's feeling and helps her recognize not only her own right to feel sad, but others' rights to the feeling, too. The same is true for positive emotions: "You have a right to feel proud of what you've done" doubly rewards a child for the actions that led to a good feeling.

Offer positive intervention. Respond to a child's fears, anxieties, anger, and frustration with empathy. Don't let him have to handle a frightening feeling alone. The child who's afraid of the dark and who's made to stay in a dark room while crying himself to sleep, doesn't learn to overcome his fear. He learns that his feelings don't matter. On the contrary, the child who's given a night-light, perhaps, and a reassuring hug learns to cope and to transcend his fears. Bribing a child out of a feeling only serves to confuse the issue. "If you stop crying, I'll buy you candy," does nothing to alleviate the feelings that brought on the tears, but teaches a child to trade his feelings for stuff.

> **READ MORE ABOUT IT**
>
> *Emotional Intelligence,* by Daniel Goleman, Ph.D. (Bantam)

Part 3:

Helping Children Develop Positive Learning Habits

40 Dealing with Procrastination

Help your child see the rewards of getting a job done.

Maybe you'd like to read this later. . . . If you're a procrastinator, chances are good that your child will be one, too. So says Noach Milgram, Ph.D., in a study done at Rhodes College in Memphis. When interviewing 365 seventh-, eighth-, and ninth-grade students and their parents, Milgram found that the procrastinating adolescents in the sample were more likely to have parents who were stallers, who filled their kids' lives with delays and frantic catch-ups—such as putting off getting ready for camp until the day before it begins and then tearing around town to find the needed items, or simply showing up late for school pick-ups and other events.

Unlearning the *desire* to put off unpleasant tasks is not easy. But learning to ignore that desire and go forward in spite of it *can* be learned:

Find good reasons to do it. Whatever "it" is, the procrastinator has good reasons for putting it off. Help your child see the rewards of getting a job done: He'll be able to stop thinking about it; he'll have time to devote to other, more pleasurable activities; he will avoid feeling stressed, guilty, angry, and all sorts of negative things he feels while the job hovers undone over his head.

170

Break it down. Writing a book report is a big job, and if all parts of it are left to the Sunday night before it's due, the task becomes overwhelming. Help your child make a list of the components—choosing the book, reading the book, chapter by chapter, deciding on the approach to take, writing an outline, drafting it, revising it, writing the final version. Encourage her to assign a reasonable amount of time to each step.

Set a schedule. The due date is not enough for the procrastinator. She needs interim dates: Read chapters 1–4 Monday; chapters 5–10 Tuesday; write notes about what I'd like the book report to say on Wednesday; write the outline on Thursday; the draft on Friday; the revision on Saturday; and the final version on Sunday.

Work in bursts. Few people have 4 hours at a time to devote to any single project, particularly one that's not fun. Help your child get in the habit of using bits and pieces of downtime—waiting for the bus or at the dentist's office—to accomplish portions of the job.

Work in rewards. Also help your child get in the habit of giving himself small rewards for each segment of the job he accomplishes. For example, "After reading chapter 4, I'll watch *Friends* on TV." "After writing the revision, I'll meet Matt for some basketball."

Plan for some mistakes and determine ways of coping. Few jobs get done without taking some missteps that require backtracking and redoing. Tossing in the towel after a mistake undoes all the work already invested. Help your child develop a strategy for dealing with inevitable frustrations, such as "When this project gets me down, I'll take a quick walk around the block to calm myself."

41 Handling Frustration

No child who's just learning to walk gives up after his first tumble. Instinctively, the toddler pushes himself back up. Falling down, he knows, is a necessary price to pay for learning to walk and then run. As the list of goals grows with a child, the need to handle frustrations and disappointments grows, too. Help him along by teaching:

Cope, don't mope. When a child is frustrated to the point of lashing out angrily or giving up, he needs reminders that frustration and disappointment are part of the human condition. They are not personal. They are not global. They are not forever.

When a child suffers a disappointment, such as failing to make the soccer team, instead of trying to *make* him feel better, which will probably backfire, offer ways to cope so that he can make *himself* feel better. Help him recognize his feelings: "I know you're disappointed." Help him find specific reasons for his upset: "You worked hard, but didn't get the result you wanted." Work on coping skills: "You can keep practicing so that you're in a better position next year." You can help him be specific about his skill level:

"Most of the other players have been playing for three years and you just started this year. Most of them are also a year older. Perhaps you just need more time and practice." You can add, "You've always enjoyed soccer. Not making the team doesn't have to make you stop liking it. Give yourself a few days before you decide how you want to handle it. In the meantime, call a friend and find something else to do right now that you enjoy."

Set small goals. When a child gives up, sometimes it's because the job seems too big, so help him break it up into smaller, more doable steps. The child who's struggling to learn to divide fractions may be overwhelmed by a homework page showing twenty problems. Suggest that he try one and see how that goes. When he's finished one, he's ready to try problem number 2 and so on. If he can't finish the whole assignment at once, that's okay.

Let her fight her own battles. Saving a child from disappointment and frustration is impossible. Help her see that just as her frustrations are her own, so must the solutions be her own. Only when a child has experienced overcoming frustrations can she apply the lesson the next time. If you rescue her, she'll doubt her own ability to save herself.

Give practice in optimism. Point out examples from your life, theirs, or any other heroic figure who managed to get past frustration and achieve success.

Help her see that just as her frustrations are her own, so must the solutions be her own.

42 Sidestepping Perfectionism

There's a Chinese proverb that says, "The perfect is the enemy of the good." Since perfection is an unattainable goal to all but a few Olympic gymnasts, learning to let go of unrealistic expectations allows the good to surface. If your child equates lack of perfection with failure:

Keep tabs on accomplishments. Perfectionist children forget that yesterday they did something well. They focus on the job at hand as the one that will make or break their reputations. These kids need reminders that no one accomplishment—or failure—is their last.

Apply time limits. When a child won't volunteer to give up rejecting, correcting, and redoing his work, give him an out: "I know you want your science project to be perfect, but no matter where you are with it at 8 p.m., that's when you have to stop."

Teach kids to put themselves in their audience's position. "If your best friend just completed that painting would you tell her that it's awful, that it needs much more work, or that she should toss it out? Treat yourself as well as you would treat a friend."

Look for patterns. Help your child see that there might be a pattern to his striving for perfection and that if he can break the pattern, he might be kinder to himself: "I notice that whenever a project is due for English class you get very hard on yourself even though you accept your good work in other classes. Why do you think that's so?"

Weigh the evidence. Teach your child to get in the habit of stepping back every so often and evaluating where on the scale of "good" she is at that moment. If at 7 p.m. her work is "almost there"; at 8 it's "really good, but not quite perfect"; and at 11 p.m. "it's still not perfect" (but now she's also tired), was the extra effort worth the minimal increase in quality? Probably not.

Kids need reminders that no one accomplishment—or failure—is their last.

175

43 Getting Organized

Physical chaos—a messy room, the inability to find a pencil when they need it—is a good companion to mental chaos. But simply having a neat room and a half dozen perfectly sharpened pencils on hand won't help if kids don't know what to do with them. To help kids organize both their space and their brain:

Help a child know his style. It takes experience to learn how much time and energy is needed to complete an assignment. Each kid also has a personal style of working and personal needs. For one kid, studying for a spelling test, for instance, may mean setting aside 5 minutes to look over the words. For another, it may mean writing each word three times, testing himself, and having you test him, all of which takes more than 5 minutes. Some children work best seated at a table with all the materials spread out in front of them; others work best in a comfortable chair with music playing. Some work best alone; others get more done and can think more clearly with you or their friends around. Help your child learn to judge his best style by experimenting with different methods.

Assemble the necessary materials. Having to interrupt herself to sharpen a pencil, find the dictionary, call a friend for details about the assignment, and search out her notes keeps a kid away from the task at hand. Before beginning an assignment, have her put all the materials she'll need in an accessible spot.

Prioritize. Get kids in the habit of making a list and determining the order in which work can best be done for them. Teach them to consider a number of factors: Which assignments are due first? Should these be started first? Which assignments are easiest? Which are harder for me? Do I work best when I get the hard or the easy things accomplished first? Does any part of this assignment require that something must be done first? For instance, "Before I can write my history report, I have to go to the library and take out a few books on the subject."

Manage time. Learning to manage time comes with experience. A child can learn that she needs to set aside 2 hours for homework only after she sees for herself that she spends 2 hours on it to get it done. She needs to take that information and use it to plan. She can't continue to be surprised that she can't get it done by her 10 p.m. bedtime when she begins at 9:30, but instead needs to say to herself, "To finish on time, I have to start at 8." Make sure there is time for frequent breaks for kids to destress and reorganize their thoughts.

Learn tricks of the trade. There are always worthwhile shortcuts and tricks to make the most of study time. Skimming a page instead of reading every word can help a

Learning to manage time comes with experience.

177

student recall and focus on the most important information. Underlining and highlighting the most pertinent facts makes reviewing a page of dense text far easier. Reading aloud instead of silently helps many learners.

Expect success. Children can learn to say to themselves, "I will remember this," as they reread their notes before a test. They can practice saying, "I will get this done," before they sit down to do a job. Programming themselves to expect success helps them achieve it.

44 Working Hard

Thinking back to our school years, even the most scholarly among us can't remember all the details we struggled so hard to learn: the years of great battles, the list of chemical symbols, how to quote *and* spell Shakespeare.

It would be easy to conclude that all that hard work was for nothing. Kids, unconvinced of the "relevance" of a lot of their subjects, can also figure "What's the point? I'll never need this information." In some cases, of course, they are absolutely right. Few adults use the minutia of their school years on a daily basis. So was all that learning, all that studying, all that *work* really worth it?

A broader look at what life offers and what it demands gives the answer: Yes, it's worth it. Why? Well, we may never have to find the hypotenuse of a triangle, but not a day goes by when most of us don't need to overcome frustration, manage our time, accept responsibility, recover from mistakes, try again, solve a problem, and cooperate. These qualities are the rich by-product of our ability to work hard.

But if simply working hard brought us these gifts, why not just work hard only at things that matter to us? Why ever take a course in mathematics when math isn't a favorite subject? The answer to that is one that even a first-grader can appreciate: The more we know, the more choices we have. At its best, an education and the hard work that goes into an education provide us with choices: How will I earn my living? How will I spend my leisure time? How will I vote? Where will I live? Without the tools to make the choices, our options are severely limited. A good education may not guarantee that we achieve all that we want to in life; a lack of a good education, however, pretty much guarantees that we won't. To help kids persevere:

Connect effort to achievement. More than saying, "nice try" for every effort, parents need to emphasize that the difference between success and failure is work. Researcher Carol Dweek of Columbia University found that kids who give up on school are those who feel helpless to change their condition. They attributed others' success to those kids being "smarter," which, of course, led them to label themselves as less able. Kids with the very same IQ, however, who believed that their input affected their achievement, worked harder and, therefore, did better. The message we need to give is, "Keep trying."

Introduce examples of persistence paying off. In Dweek's study, she gave some students who didn't value effort stories to read that demonstrated how triumph followed hard work. She gave others in this group books on heroes who attributed their success to luck. Subsequently, the kids exposed to the idea of hard work chose more challenging work themselves and willingly worked harder than they had in the past. Their level of success went way up. Kids from the second group continued to feel helpless and continued to underachieve.

Focus on learning, not on grades. When a child succeeds at a task, compliment her strategy, not her grade. For instance, when she brings home a math test for which she has earned an A, instead of saying, "Wow! You're so smart," ask, "How did you figure this problem out?" This gives her a chance to repeat her good performance and to use this skill again and again, even on tests for which she might not earn an A. On the other hand, when a child bemoans her grade, say, "You seem upset. Have you figured out where you made mistakes?" This gives her a chance to see that "I divided numbers instead of multiplying to find the common denominator." Now she's learned what she needs for her next test.

Allow some errors to pass without your judgment. When reviewing your child's work, don't feel compelled to correct every misspelling or handwriting failure. You'll only reduce his motivation.

Don't invest too much of yourself in your child's performance. His grades are his, not yours. When parents express anxiety about their kids' need to study for a test or complete an assignment, they take the job of worrying about these things out of the kids' hands.

Don't be afraid to nag a little. If you're too casual, too removed, from your child's schoolwork, she'll conclude that it doesn't really matter whether she does it or not. Show that while the work is up to her, you're not completely out of the picture.

When parents express anxiety about their kids' need to study for a test or complete an assignment, they take the job of worrying about these things out of the kids' hands.

45 Setting Goals

Goals are dreams with feet. To dream of a future remains a dream, but to work toward it brings it into focus and within reach. Not everyone reaches their goals, but few arrive in the place they want to be without having aimed for it.

Help your child define her goal. To help your child reach a goal, she must first define it. A person who wants to be a doctor, for instance, can find out what school subjects she should take now to prepare her for medical school, even if that's a decade away.

Support dreams. Don't let your own feelings of limitation interfere with your child's goal. Some kids do indeed grow up to be stars of stage and screen, senators, and world-class athletes. Don't make fun of a goal, no matter how remote it might seem.

Use visualization. Suggest that your child ask himself, "What do I look like accepting my gold medal?" or "What will it feel like to be aboard the first manned spaceship to

Mars?" Being able to imagine himself succeeding in reaching his goal brings success closer.

Find mentors. Whatever a child's goals are, there's someone out there who's a master in that arena. Help the budding scientist connect to a university researcher who can steer her in the right direction and connect her to others who can also help her realize her goals.

Don't let your own feelings of limitation interfere with your child's goal.

Part 4:

UNDERSTANDING AND ENHANCING YOUR CHILD'S SCHOOL EXPERIENCE

46 My Child's Learning Style

In scattered classrooms around the country, there's a quiet revolution taking place. Its premise? *All* children are smart, and the job of teachers and parents is to help each child find the style of learning that will allow his or her unique intelligence to shine through.

The teachers in these classrooms are putting the "theory of multiple intelligences" (MI) into practice. The MI theory, developed by Howard Gardner and his colleagues at Harvard University, moved into the mainstream with the publication of *7 Kinds of Smart* by Thomas Armstrong. Since the publication of that book, an eighth "smart"—learning through any combination of the seven—has been added. Basically, MI advocates challenge traditional notions of intelligence as well as the IQ and other tests that claim to rate intelligence. They point out that traditional teaching and testing focus only on two of the seven intelligences people possess: language and logic skills. So a child who *doesn't* learn in a style that relies on language and logic skills is labeled as deficient.

According to Armstrong, it's the teaching methods, not the kids, that are faulty. "We try to remake children to get them to learn in *our* way, when, in fact, we must remake the way we teach to fit the children," he protests. "Only when we recognize that different kids learn in different ways and that all ways of learning are okay are we going to be truly in the business of educating kids."

The Seven Kinds of Smart

As the title of Armstrong's book suggests, there are a number of styles of learning—distinct intelligences—that students bring with them to the task of learning. Using verbal abilities and logic skills—the traditional reading, writing, and arithmetic—account for just two of these intelligences, what Armstrong calls "Word Smart" and "Logic Smart." The other intelligences, say the MI researchers, are equally important, and to ignore them is to risk that a child work against rather than with his own intelligence. So the question for teachers and parents is this: How do we match a child's learning style to what is being taught? A look at a typical classroom lesson about the Civil War can shed some light on how the theory can be put into practice, using each of the intelligences:

Word Smart. *This learner learns by listening, reading, speaking, and writing.* Reading and hearing about the conflict and preparing a written or an oral report would serve this child's ability to grasp the material.

Logic Smart. *This learner learns by using number facts and scientific principles, and by observing and experimenting.* A classroom discussion that included "what if . . ." questions would spark this student's understanding of the material. He would also learn by using props to recreate battle scenes and by creating diagrams of Civil War battle strategies.

Different kids learn in different ways.

Picture Smart. *She sees what casual observers miss, can visualize, and can use these powers to create images and concrete structures.* This child can "draw on" her talent by studying paintings, photographs, films, and other images and by being encouraged to express ideas in visual ways, perhaps creating a diorama or a model landscape of a battle scene.

Music Smart. *This learner is inclined to grasp information that's presented melodically.* His understanding is enhanced when materials are presented in songs, metered poetry, or jingles, and absorbs information when music—just about any music—is playing in the background. Such a child might create a musical piece to represent an understanding of various Civil War events.

Body Smart. *This child learns in physical ways, through the senses and through movement.* A body-smart learner may come to a deeper understanding of her Civil War lesson once she is in motion, for instance while walking home from school and allowing thoughts to wander. In the classroom, she benefits from physical experiences—performing in a skit or handling artifacts to absorb their feel and textures.

People Smart. *This child learns as part of a social process.* He thrives when working with others, listening to different viewpoints, and having a chance to express his own opinion. Engaging in discussions or working on a project with other students about the Civil War serves him well.

Self Smart. *This learner learns through introspection.* In learning about the Civil War, she incorporates personal feelings about the events into the lesson and might create a fictionalized diary of what it feels like to be a Civil War soldier.

All kids display each of these learning styles to a greater or lesser degree, Armstrong explains. But each student has a natural inclination to draw upon one or more to learn most readily, he emphasizes. He notes, too, that a learner's preferred style this year may be supplanted by another next year. "Almost all toddlers," he says, "are Body Smart, learning by touching, feeling, and doing. As kids grow and change, other strengths emerge." Likewise, culture plays a part in which native strengths flourish and others may go underground. "Almost all cultures," Armstrong notes, "pass on knowledge musically from one generation to the next." For example, in our culture, kids learn their ABCs by singing them because it works and because we're comfortable allowing young children to learn in this playful manner. As kids move along the school path, we use music less and less as a means of teaching. Says Armstrong: "That's sad for all children, but for some, it's a real tragedy."

What Parents and Teachers Can Do

Teachers and parents might be relieved to know that kids can benefit from using MI without a complete overhaul of traditional education. "Incorporating MI theory into the classroom requires a shift in attitude," Armstrong stresses. "With MI, we work from a child's strengths, rather than trying to compensate for weaknesses." It is not necessary,

MI adherents say, to teach every new concept in a way that draws upon each learning style in every single lesson. A lesson about the Gettysburg Address, for instance, might draw upon Word, Picture, People, and Self Smarts, while a lesson about a particular battle might be taught from a Logic Smart and a Body Smart perspective. "What matters," says Thomas Hoerr, principal of the New City School in St. Louis, Missouri, which has incorporated the MI theory into the curriculum, "is that over the course of a day, each child is able to bring his or her unique learning style into play."

What's your role as a parent? Amstrong suggests becoming what he calls a "cooperative advocate" for your child at school. If, for example, your Picture Smart kid just "isn't getting it" in math class, say to the teacher, "I know my child really learns by drawing. Are there ways to let him use drawing in his math work?" If the teacher insists that your child learn math traditionally, then work with him at home, giving him opportunities to learn comfortably and with your full support.

Armstrong also reminds us all of the danger in labeling a child "lazy" or "slow." Likewise, applying labels such as "artistic learner" with a strong adhesive defeats the overall purpose of MI, which is to broaden, not limit, each learner's potential. "Let children use their special gifts," he urges, "but also encourage the exploration of all the intelligences. That's the road to discovery."

47 Homework

Homework theory: Homework is the child's job.

Homework fact: Homework, like the flu, can infect even the healthiest of families with chills, fits, and waves of nausea.

If homework worked the way it was supposed to, kids would remember to bring home their assignments, read the book before the report was due, and gather the necessary research materials before the 11th hour. In real life, assignments disappear mysteriously between school and home, and kids try almost anything to avoid doing it. A 20-minute assignment stretches into hours as kids declare themselves "too tired" or "too hungry." "I have a headache!" "It's too hard!" "It's dumb!" some cry. Like it or not, parents are dragged screaming into the homework hole. There are ways out:

Support the need for homework. Even parents can decry the usefulness of homework. But understanding its purpose—to review learning, to ingrain good work habits, to teach responsibility, to help kids overcome frustration—can help put parents on the positive side of homework. Be matter-of-fact in any response to a kid's pleas to "write a note and say I was sick." Instead try, "Homework is just one of those things that have to get done. Let's figure out the best way to do it with the least amount of pain. Then you'll be able to do whatever else you'd rather be doing."

Know the teacher's policies. What does your child's teacher expect? How much time should it take? Are you supposed to sign off on completed work? Test your child on what he's done? Correct her spelling? Limit yourself to what the teacher wants. The teacher won't know what your child can accomplish if you've corrected all of her errors. If you notice that most math answers are wrong and that your child is having difficulty with the work, for instance, write a brief note to the teacher, stating that the assignment presented a challenge and ask for guidance on what additional help you or the teacher can offer.

Monitor assignments. Help your young child get in the habit of looking at his list of assignments with you. This will allow you to note any long-range ones ahead of time.

Have materials available. In addition to the books your child carts back and forth to school, make sure the tools she's likely to need are near her workstation.

Respect your child's style. Some kids need peace and solitude. Others work best with friends or family around. Some have the energy immediately after school; others need to chill out a bit first. Some find that working in a straightback chair works best for math, while English homework gets done best sprawled out on the bed. There's no one right time or place for every learner. Let your child figure out what works for him.

HOMEWORK TIMELINES

The National PTA recommends the following time frames as appropriate for kids in each grade. (times do not include setting up or dawdling.):

From kindergarten to third grade—no more than 20 minutes per day

From fourth to sixth grade—20 to 40 minutes per day

From seventh to 12th grade—one to two hours per day

Establish ground rules. While his style can be his own, you can set the perameters. Knowing what you expect in terms of neatness, efficiency, time, and quality helps a child aim for those standards. Involve your child in setting the rules as much as possible, but, once established, be consistent about enforcing them.

Watch your words. Telling your child to "quit whining and get on with it" doesn't help anyone. Instead offer confident encouragement: "I know it's hard, but you've done hard work before and you can do it again."

Direct your child to break a big job into smaller parts. Offer to review the material with your child, helping her see that a large math problem, for example, is made up of smaller problems that she has mastered. Encourage her to write down the steps for later reference.

Help him get started. Sometimes just seeing a blank page freezes a child in his tracks. Sit with him as he tackles the first line in a report or the first math problem. Once something is on paper, he's more able to keep going. Brainstorm with him for ideas for projects and ways of approaching the work.

Don't help too much. Sticking around to help from beginning to end tells your child that she's incapable of handling the assignment herself. Most likely, she's not. And if she is that's an issue to discuss with her teacher.

ON-LINE HOMEWORK HELPERS

FOR GENERAL HOMEWORK HELP

Both America On Line and CompuServe offer kids' tutoring rooms and message boards, on which students can post questions that are answered by teachers contracted by the services. The teachers can also direct kids to other areas on the Internet for further research. Kids can also access the following address on the Net for general help—http://trfn.clpgh.org.Education/K12/homework.html

In addition to these general sites, these offer help in specific subject areas:

To view historic documents—http://www.law.emory.edu. Then type in a keyword, such as Constitution.

To view current-events articles contained in *Time* magazine or *USA Today*—http://pathfinder.com/time. Or http://www.usatoday.com

To find the right science book-http://www.plcme.lib.nc.us/is/bibliographies/sfpbis94.html

To prepare a science project—http://www.isd77.k12mn.us/resources/cf/steps.html

---

Keep distractions to a minimum. It's just not fair to be watching The Simpsons yourself on TV, while telling the kids to stick to their homework. Nor can a child concentrate when he's told to clear the table of schoolbooks so dinner can be served. Allowing younger siblings to tear through a school child's workplace also disrupts the focus. As much as possible, respect your child's efforts to stick to the job by respecting his space.

READ MORE ABOUT IT

The Homework Plan, by Linda Sonna (Berkley)
MegaSkills, by the Home and School Institute (Houghton Mifflin)
Making the Grade, by Ginger E. Black (Lyle Stuart Books)
How to Help Your Child with Homework, by Marguerite Radencich and Jean Shay Schumm
    (Free Spirit Publishing)
The Homework Plan: A Parent's Guide to Helping Kids Excel, by Linda Sonna (Berkley)
*Taming the Homework Monster: How to Make Homework a Positive Learning Experience for
    Your Child,* by Ellen Klavan (Poseidon Press)
Scholastic's A+ Junior Guide to Studying, by Louise Colligan (Scholastic)

Offer rewards. Offer nontangibles for completed assignments: playing a game with you, choosing the family's dessert, or an extra bedtime story. Some children respond well to star charts, on which they can record a full week of homework success to earn them a special outing or other reward.

Find shortcuts. If reading a 160-page book about the Civil War is overwhelming your fifth-grader, suggest that she read a junior version of a book on the same subject. She'll still learn quite a bit. Get tape recordings of Shakespeare's plays to help get your high-schooler through *Hamlet.* Let your child use a calculator for her math homework, once you and she are assured that she understands the basic concepts. Encourage your

It's often easier for kids to accept help from others than from their parents.

child with poor handwriting to use a wordprocessing and spell checker program on the computer. Let her trace a map instead of trying to draw it freehand.

Get outside help. See if your child's school offers a peer tutoring program or if there's an older student you can hire to explain the finer points of geometry to your son. It's often easier for kids to accept help from others than from their critical parents.

Back off. If all your good intentions and efforts don't pay off and your child doesn't respond responsibly to her homework assignments, let her take the consequences.

48 Parent-Teacher Conferences

(Mom and) Pop Quiz

The note arrives home, alerting you to the upcoming parent-teacher conference. You:

a) panic, remembering the dread you felt long ago when you were the student and your parents were about to find out the truth about what really happened in the lunchroom that day you came home wearing a gallon of tomato sauce

b) feel anxious, recalling your last meeting with your child's teacher, who suggested that your progeny was no prodigy

c) lose the note, pretty much guaranteeing that you'll forget the meeting

d) mark your calendar and make a list of questions to ask your child before the meeting and questions for his or her teacher at the meeting

e) practice your stride and prepare to gloat over what's sure to be a wonderful visit

Visiting your child's teacher at school brings out different emotions in different people. Your own school experiences are likely to come flooding back; the better your memories of school, the more likely you are to feel positive about the upcoming encounter. Likewise, if your child's experiences are generally good, you'll be expecting a pleasant report. If, however, either you or your kid has had trouble in the past, the upcoming visit can be fraught with anxiety. Just thinking about squeezing yourself into those too-small chairs for a face-to-face with a teacher can cause some parents to break out in a cold sweat. What are the secrets to making the most of your time with that other important adult in your child's life? Start with answer (d) above. Then, do *your* homework; suggested assignments are below.

> The real point of the conference is not about fixing problems but about avoiding them.

Most importantly, remember that the school conference, though an important juncture in the school year, is not your only opportunity to become involved in your child's education. It's not even the best one. Throughout the school year, be sure to make your commitment to your child's education known through visits with teachers and administrators, by making sure your child attends to his or her work, and by volunteering when you can. Then the school conference will be what it was meant to be—what one mother of a ninth-grader called "a well-child check-up, instead of an emergency room visit." The real point of the conference, after all, is not about fixing problems but about avoiding them. It's really about sharing—sharing your child with a teacher, your own time with your child's school, and the teacher's comments with your child to create a partnership that will serve everyone.

Do *Your* Homework

As you would for any business meeting, come prepared for your meeting with your child's teacher:

- *Enlist your child's help in evaluating his or her school performance.* Ask your child, "How do you think you're doing? Is there anything you'd like me to ask or tell your teacher?" If school policy allows, consider setting up a three-way conference, so that your child can be part of the discussion.
- *Know what the teacher's expectations* are for academic and social performance and ask if your child is meeting, exceeding, or falling short of these expectations. Look beyond grades and other objective measures of performance to find out how your child appears to be doing socially and emotionally, too.
- *Know how your child is being graded*—by classroom participation, by homework assignments, by test scores, by his portfolio. Find out how you can best keep up-to-date on his or her work.
- *Ask the teacher what he or she expects your role as a parent to be.* Are you expected to review homework, help with assignments, sign reports? Be sure to ask questions if you don't understand something the teacher tells you, and ask for specific examples if a teacher makes a statement that you don't understand.
- *Find out what help within the school system is available* and how you can go about getting it, if your child requires additional help in meeting academic and behavior standards. If in-school help is not available, find out where you can go outside the school.
- *Know the professional structure of your child's school.* If you wish to discuss a teacher's evaluation of your child with another school official, to whom can you turn? Talk to the head of the parents' association to learn the usual protocol for your child's school.

Teachers benefit from your insights into what makes your kid tick.

- *Share important information about your child with his or her teacher.* There's more to your child than his or her school performance. What are his interests? What are her hobbies? What are your child's goals in life? Is anything going on at home that affects the student's school performance? Teachers benefit from your insights into what makes your kid tick.

- *Watch your phrasing and your body language.* In an excellent audiotape, "Who Knows What About Your Child?" by Achievement, Inc., (part of the *When Parents Face the School* series), coauthor Dr. Judy-Arin Krupp recommends that parents use language that supports their child and helps the teacher see the student in a more positive light. For instance, rather than saying, "She never pays attention," try, "We're working on helping her pay attention." Dr. Krupp also stresses the importance of maintaining a cooperative posture throughout the meeting. Rather than being defensive, ask for the teacher's recommendations on solving any problems. Offer your own suggestions. Talk with, not at, one another. If you disagree on what's best for a child, such as whether or not a child should repeat a grade, find ways to be cooperative rather than confrontational. Get together to make it work.

- *If possible, have both parents attend the conference.* Sometimes one parent must stay home with the kids while the other attends meetings. Sometimes parents are divorced and only the custodial parent gets involved in school business. Whatever the circumstances, remember that the point of the conference is to benefit your child's school career. The more insights about your child that the teacher can hear and the more support your child can receive from those who have an impact on his or her life, the better.

- *Share the contents of your conference with your child.* Be sure to share all positive comments about your child's performance with him. And phrase the "needs improvement" portion of the report in a way that will engender cooperation. For instance, "No TV until your math grades are up" is unlikely to result in much commitment to change. A better approach would be to say, "I know you're having difficulty with math. Your teacher, you, and I need to work out a plan so that you can do better." Then ask your child for suggestions, offer your own, and check back with the teacher as you all develop a strategy.

49 My Child is Underachieving or Dislikes School

My favorite T-shirt reads, "I yell because I care." My daughter doesn't find it nearly as amusing as I do, but my friends have been asking me where they can purchase one. For all of us parents, yelling, we concur, almost always involves schoolwork. We want our kids to try harder than they're trying, to adjust their attitudes, to choose work over play, sometimes to do more than they can reasonably do. It's a tall order.

There are a number of reasons that some kids resist school or don't operate on full throttle. Not all of the reasons, in fact, point to any deficit in the kids. Perhaps, for starters, we could all yell a bit less.

Before School Problems Start

Find the best match. The school environment that's right for one child may chafe like an ill-fitting pair of shoes on another. Fitting your child's learning style, his personality, and his academic and social needs to a particular school or teacher is essential, though not always easy. Where there is a choice of classrooms or schools, consider all options. Don't limit your younger child's options to his older siblings' school. Their needs may be vastly different. Talk to school administrators, other parents, and your child to determine which teaching method best suits a particular student—an open mixed-age classroom, a traditional classroom, a gifted program, a program that focuses on art and music, or another option. Before determining that a private school is financially out of reach, check out tuition-assistance and scholarship programs. Within your public school system, take advantage of all offered testing and evaluation programs that can help you ascertain your best choices within and outside your district.

Choose the right grade at the right age/stage of development. Over the last twenty years or so, there's been a tremendous downward shift in the early-learning curriculum. What was once taught in first grade—from simple math to reading—has become the staple of kindergarten classrooms. It's not because kindergartners have suddenly gotten smarter. Rather it's because kindergarteners, with years of nursery school under their belts, more frequently enter school having already accomplished the socialization skills that once predominated the kindergarten curriculum. In addition, some parents opt to keep their 5-year-olds in nursery school (or the more recently renamed "pre-kindergarten") classrooms rather than move them into kindergarten.

Given these new circumstances, the traditional 5-year-old kindergartener is often at a disadvantage. If she can do the work, she's fine academically, though she may lack the social skills of her older classmates. Or, if she can't do the work of a 6-year-old, she begins to feel less capable than she is. Nevertheless, she may move along into first grade, fully a year behind her "peers" in her development. Eventually, usually by third grade, she either catches up or falls further behind and then may, at last, be placed with her age-mates by repeating the grade. In the meantime, her self-esteem has unnecessarily taken some lumps.

The best solution to determining when your child should enter school is to consider not just her age, but the age of others in her class, her own level of development, and the structure of the curriculum. If possible, consider a mixed-aged classroom, which works well for most younger learners, allowing 5-, 6-, 7- and 8-year-olds to progress at their own paces from kindergarten through second grade before settling into the more structured upper grades.

If your child is entering a single-grade kindergarten classroom, realize that, in general, the older members of the class are better able to handle the academic and social demands better than the younger ones. If you're unsure if your 5-year-old is ready, meet with the teachers, preferably along with your child. Be clear with your child that she is not being judged, but that your job is to determine when is the best time for her to start kindergarten. Many children benefit from an extra year of preschool, particularly if their development in either academic or social arenas does not match the school's expectations for a kindergartener.

On the other hand, many 5-year-olds are ready, academically and socially, for the experience. If your 5-year-old is ready, but the school's policy is to restrict kindergarten admission to 6-year-olds, work at home and with his preschool teacher to provide the stimulation he needs.

Demonstrate a good parental attitude. A study conducted by Laurence Steinberg of Temple University and Bradford Brown of the University of Wisconsin, showed that the only factor that held equal sway with friends' attitudes in determining a child's school motivation is her parents' attitude. Those parents who become involved and stay involved in their child's school life boost her performance. Those who disengage from their child's schoolwork give the message that schoolwork doesn't matter much.

What parents communicate in words to the child means little if parents simultaneously show a disrespectful attitude toward the school or teachers. For instance, saying, "School is important," is easily overridden if your child hears you telling another parent that his teacher is a jerk. Speaking disrepectfully to the teacher or other school personnel also undermines the school's authority.

Get help. If your child is struggling or is bored, get help early on. Waiting is likely to increase the problem. Make sure your child understands that your aim is to correct the problem, not fix him.

If a Child Dislikes School

Most kids, at one time or another, declare that they don't like school. For some, it's more than just a cool statement to impress friends; they usually have good reasons.

Academics. A child who struggles unsuccessfully academically cannot enjoy the place that regularly diminishes his sense of self. Neither can the child who faces few intellectual challenges. If your child is seriously mismatched with his school and/or grade

Those parents who become involved and stay involved in their child's school life boost her performance.

level, discuss your options with his teacher or other administrator to see if the curriculum and/or teaching methods can be adjusted to serve him better. The child who is developmentally out of sync with his grade level can benefit from repeating or skipping a grade. The child who is ill-suited to the rigors of academics should not, however, be made to feel the chill of failure repeatedly and will not likely benefit from repeating a grade. In this case, the curriculum needs to be adjusted to the child's abilities. In any case when there's a mismatch and the problems can't be abated, consider moving him to another environment—another classroom or even another school.

Social life. Kids need friends at school. Friends who support learning urge a child to excel. Friends who have a low regard for schoolwork infect a child with a bad attitude. And a child who has trouble with a clique or a bully is going to be distracted. If trouble with friendships are interfering with your child's school achievement, be empathetic. Open your home to her friends and their parents, where you can monitor their interactions and provide a safe refuge (and a few pizzas). Make sure, too, that she has opportunities to know achievers through after-school and other activities.

Strategies to Improve School Performance

- If your child feigns illness to avoid going to school, encourage him to go, and agree to pick him up later if the illness continues. Most of the time, he'll manage to stick out the day. Or, if you do allow him to stay in bed for the morning, urge him to join his class later in the day.

- Create a written contract with your child, listing his responsibilities and the rewards and consequences for not meeting those responsibilities. Don't demand more—or less—than the child can handle.
- Don't expect your child to do it all alone. She needs you to help her get to bed on time, provide the tools she needs, offer encouragement, and reward honest efforts—even those that result in failure.

Five Things Not to Say When You're Helping Kids Learn

When we're attempting to teach our kids something, our frustration can easily become theirs. Certain one-liners, tossed out because we're angry at our children for not learning at the pace that suits us, can undermine all the good teaching we can do:

- *"If only you'd put as much energy into your math work as you put into these drawings. . . ."* What budding artist needs to have her great works used as a weapon against her? When we see our children pour the best of themselves into an activity that we don't value highly, it's tempting to wonder why that same energy can't be "better spent." But a phrase such as this one merely deflates a child's ego. When kids show off a talent, recognize the feat independently of their shortcomings.
- *"How come all the other kids can understand this and you can't?"* Learning—even in the social environs of a classroom—is a very personal thing. Comparing one child with another does no good. If a child is truly behind his classmates in a particular area, talk

Comparing one child with another does no good.

207

to the teacher and to him for problem-solving strategies. Don't ask a child who's having trouble with addition to take on the task of becoming a child psychologist too.

- *"What's the matter with you?"* Probably nothing until now. But after hearing this phrase, especially if it's repeated often, she's not only struggling with learning a particular skill, she also must contend with the fact that her parent thinks there's something really wrong with her.
- *"If you don't learn XYZ, you're grounded for a month."* There's always a temptation to get punitive when a child seems to be stubbornly stuck. While we're right to offer reasonable consequences for failure to carry out necessary tasks (no TV until homework is finished, for example) it's counterproductive to threaten a child when he's unable to learn what he's supposed to. Most often, when a child is stuck, he either needs more time to be ready to learn a particular skill or he needs to learn more productive study habits so that he can use the skills he already has to master new ones. Offer sticks and carrots only for behaviors that are totally within a child's control. Don't reward or punish a child for grasping or not grasping concepts.
- *"I give up."* Step back, but don't give up. Acknowledge when you're not the one to help and find someone who can do the job.

50 Letting Go

I am a terrible teacher. This self-knowledge is not something of which I'm proud, but it's the truth. It's not true in a global sense: I believe I have indeed taught my child well in matters of character, in helping her see the world as a welcoming place, and in helping her seek out her true self. But it is true when it comes to teaching her measurable things like how to ride a bike or read. Too many of our one-on-one, goal-oriented sessions have ended in tears for both of us. Not a pretty picture.

I (and she, I'm sure) have looked on with envy and admiration at those moms and dads we know who have patiently fashioned a variety of dinosaurs out of homemade clay, and who have listened, over and over and over, to their children's piano practice, offering nothing but enthusiastic encouragement. These parents have a wholly different genetic makeup, I suspect, that keeps their frustration low and their tolerance high. Or maybe they've just learned things that I haven't yet learned.

Nevertheless, I have learned that though I score high on limitations, I am still my child's first and still most important teacher. And though I haven't always been able to teach her specific skills, I have taught her (and myself) that there are reasonable ways around this limitation and that sometimes the best "teaching" I can do is to get out of the way and let someone better qualified take over. Though the cost is nearly prohibitive, I've turned her reading instruction over to a wonderful tutor, who has taught her to read. I've limited my involvement to providing the books, turning off the TV on (most) school nights, and making it possible for her to have a half hour a day to read. I've supplied stationery to encourage letter writing, and I continue to read a chapter or two a day from one of the books she enjoys hearing but isn't yet able to tackle on her own. It was not all I set out to do, but, experience showed, it was all I was able to do well.

As for the bike riding, I stopped insisting that she follow my directions and asked her to tell me how I could help. She was blunt: "Just stay out of my way and don't tell me what to do." I sat on a bench and pretended to be reading. She wobbled, never putting her feet on the pedals. I kept my frustration to myself though I was dying to cheer her on, to encourage just a bit more daring behavior on her part. On our third outing, I took my place on the bench and within about ten minutes, she went pedaling by me, shouting, "I'm a bike rider!" And she was.

As time goes on, there will be more that I can't teach her, not just because my temperament makes me ill-suited to the task but because these subjects are beyond my knowledge. I don't believe I've abdicated my responsibilities by helping her find others who are better teachers than I or by sitting on the sidelines while she figures things out for herself. I know that even if I were to teach her every skill I have and every fact I know, it would not be enough to serve her. Her own personality, likes and dislikes, talents

Sometimes the best "teaching" I can do is to get out of the way and let someone better qualified take over.

and limitations are separate from mine. She's growing up under different circumstances in different times. She most definitely (as she loves to remind me) is not me. And I am not her.

What I've learned serves me. What she learns, and how she learns it, serves her. This doesn't mean, of course, that I won't try and fail at some future lessons or try and succeed at others. It just reminds me to be on guard against assuming that I can orchestrate all of my child's successes or protect her from all failures. It means stepping back and giving her the room to learn. It means, in fact, letting go of my own inflated sense of importance. I'm just her mother, not her soul.

RESOURCES FOR PARENTS

School Match—an independent nationwide school research/consulting organization and database, which provides information to make the best local match between a school and a particular child.

Blendonview Office Park
5027 Pine Creek Drive
Westerville, OH 43081
Telephone: (614) 890-1573
e-mail: http://schoolmatch.com

Girls Incorporated—an organization that supplies training manuals to schools, classrooms, and parents on ways to deal with gender bias and other issues affecting girls.

30 East 33rd Street
New York, NY 10016
Telephone: (212) 689-3700

Make the Most of Family Time with These Peterson's Titles

The Working Parents Help Book 2nd edition

Susan Crites Price and Tom Price
How do you decide between in-home child care and a child-care center? How can you stay involved in your child's school? How can you control risky behavior? This accessible quick-read covers the range of day-to-day challenges faced by those juggling kids and careers. Offers strategies, expert advice, and software to help parents cope with ongoing issues.
ISBN 1-56079-579-4, 400 pp., 7 x 9, $16.95 pb

100 Things You Can Do To Keep Your Family Together . . .

When It Sometimes Seems Like the Whole World Is Trying to Pull It Apart
Marge Kennedy
Rediscovering your ancestors and family history. Making a family time capsule. Playing hooky with your kids. There are 97 more ideas for togetherness in this delightful book for the busy modern family. Filled with thoughtful suggestions about ways you can enhance family togetherness, it's practical, realistic, and, most of all, fun.
ISBN 1-56079-340-6, 112 pp., 9 x 6, $5.95 pb

Available at Fine Bookstores Near You
Or Order Direct
Call: 800-338-3282 Fax: 609-243-9150

P Peterson's P.O. Box 2123, Princeton, NJ 08543-2123

Praise for the first edition: "... a must for the two-career moms and dads."
—*Parents' Choice*

Winner of the Parents' Choice Award

AS SEEN ON OPRAH

THE CLASSIC FOR WORKING MOMS AND DADS, NOW EXPANDED AND UPDATED

THE WORKING PARENTS HELP BOOK New Edition

Practical advice for dealing with the day-to-day challenges of kids and careers

Tom Price

100 THINGS You Can Do TO KEEP YOUR FAMILY TOGETHER...
when it sometimes seems like the whole world is trying to pull it apart
MARGE KENNEDY

"... offers fun-to-do suggestions for enhancing family togetherness."
—*Work & Family Life*

Visit Peterson's on the Internet **http://www.petersons.com**